VANCOUVER'S
MOST HAUNTED

T0160177

Edited by Renée Layberry
Cover and interior design by Sydney Barnes
Cover photo by Vicki Ng of Vixxi Pix Photography

CATALOGUING DATA AVAILABLE FROM LIBRARY AND ARCHIVES CANADA
ISBN: 9781771513180 (SOFTCOVER)
ISBN: 9781771513197 (ELECTRONIC)

TouchWood Editions acknowledges that the land on which we live and work is within the traditional territories of the Lkwungen (Esquimalt and Songhees), Malahat, Pacheedaht, Scia'new, T'Sou-ke and W̱SÁNEĆ (Pauquachin, Tsartlip, Tsawout, Tseycum) peoples.

We acknowledge the financial support of the Government of Canada through the Canada Book Fund and the Canada Council for the Arts, and of the Province of British Columbia through the British Columbia Arts Council and the Book Publishing Tax Credit.

Nothing ever becomes real
till it is experienced.
—John Keats

To all those who have experienced the unexplained,
this book is for you.

CONTENTS

INTRODUCTION

V ANCOUVER IS, WITHOUT A DOUBT, ONE OF THE LOVELIEST cities in the world. Its diverse cultural population, stunning natural attributes, and enviable position on the west coast of Canada make it an incredibly attractive place to be.

As with any wonderful city, Vancouver comes with layers of history, and that history leaves traces. Sometimes you'll find those traces in buildings, or at other times in parks; once in a while, those traces are found in places with ambiguous origins.

Ghost stories from city to city often share commonalities. Theatres, hospitals, and hotels seem to retain energy in a tighter, heavier way than other places. Sometimes a spectral presence will linger where a tragedy took place; at other times it's simply that the residual energy of people who existed for generations still resonates in a certain location. And then, once in a while, there's a haunting for no reason at all. Much of the time, ghost stories are aligned with older places with an identifiable story attached, but that's not always the case.

As you will see in *Vancouver's Most Haunted*, ghosts do what they want. They appear in different ways, and sometimes they can only be perceived through specific senses. In my years of collecting and sharing ghost stories, and as a Ghostly Walk tour guide in Victoria, British Columbia, I've learned that most ghosts want connection— to be heard, to be acknowledged. I'm sure if I was stuck alone in a house for seventy years and someone who could sense me came in, I'd be quite anxious to communicate! Ghosts are not there to scare us, generally, but when we encounter them, of course we get frightened because we don't know what is going on—especially when we've decided we're not the type to believe in ghosts. Some of my favourite stories involve those who were previously skeptical, because they're always so surprised when they have an encounter and discover they've been wrong.

While writing this book, I was delighted to learn more about Vancouver as a city and its history over the last hundred years, and I developed a new appreciation for the City of Vancouver's being situated on the traditional territories of the Musqueam, Squamish, and Tsleil-Waututh—the traditional unceded territory of the Coast Salish people. For these reasons and more, I am utterly convinced that Vancouver is fascinating and exceptional.

I am so grateful to all of the fantastic individuals, paranormal groups, and fellow tour guides in Vancouver who took the time to communicate with me, either by reaching out or responding when I reached out to them. Thank you. When it comes to learning ghost stories, it all comes down to the people and the history. That's what I love most. The true beauty of ghost stories is that they belong to history—their own history, on their own terms. Our job, as those who care to listen, is to learn and share these stories, to keep them alive, to pass them on from generation to generation. It's an honour and privilege to be part of that chain.

Throughout the book I have changed people's names. Anyone who asked for their name to be withheld has been given a pseudonym. Where the story involves private residences, the details have been kept vague to protect the privacy of the people involved. I'd like to add that the stories and experiences shared in this book are based on the author's collection of sources, including individuals whose experiences have led them to believe they have encountered phenomena of some kind or another. The stories are meant to entertain, and neither the publisher nor the author claim that these stories represent fact. Additionally, it is not my intention to influence anyone's beliefs;

instead, my hope is that these stories will inspire, thrill, delight, and comfort.

I invite you to get comfortable wherever you are (just make sure the room is well lit!) and enjoy this offering of stories from Vancouver, British Columbia—Canada's prettiest city—and come to know its history, its people, and its ghosts.

VANCOUVER'S THEATRES

WHEN I LEAD THE GHOSTLY WALK TOURS IN VICTORIA, which I really enjoy doing, guests often have questions. One of the most popular questions is, What is the most haunted place? I always have the same response: No matter where you live, if you want to find a ghost, start with hotels, hospitals, and theatres.

Vancouver is no exception to this rule. There are several old, preserved theatres still around, and at least three of them have their very own ghosts.

Why theatres? Well, just think of the amount of energy being put out by the performers onstage—and not only that, but the reaction and energy of the audience in response to that performance. This is a place where people dream, work tirelessly, and fight to express themselves; performers and staff come together to make something special happen. Theatres have their own kind of magic, so much so that we go there and pay money to be distracted or to feel like part of something bigger. In this setting, we can experience life from another perspective or have a shared musical experience that can only happen by being present in that space. It's almost as if a spell is cast when a performance begins, and we willingly fall under its power. That power, without a doubt, seems to linger and permeate the buildings in which it is unleashed.

Some theatre traditions are superstitious and open to the presence of the paranormal. It is well known, for example, that one must never say "good luck" to a performer about to go on stage; instead they are told to "break a leg." The name of *Macbeth* should never be uttered in the theatre, but should be referred to instead as The Scottish Play.

And, of course, there is the tradition of the ghost light—usually just a bare, low-wattage bulb left at centre stage when the rest of the theatre has been powered down and everyone has gone home. Some say the ghost light is there to ensure that anyone moving through the theatre will be able to see the edges of the stage and avoid a nasty fall; others say the ghost light either keeps the ghosts at bay by lighting the stage, or leaves enough light on the stage for the resident spirits to have their time there, before vacating when the living performers arrive. In any case, most theatres have a ghost light.

Whatever the reasons, whatever the superstitions, and whatever the stories, theatres seem to be exceptionally good at claiming resident ghosts—long-departed performers, staff, and patrons who never seem to want to leave the place that brought them so much joy.

THE STANLEY

T HE STANLEY WAS BUILT, IN 1930, AS A DESIGNATED MOVIE
theatre and it was a huge success for fifty years. Continued
improvements in sound and projection meant that the Stanley
enjoyed a long career as the place to see blockbuster movies for many
people throughout the region.

Naturally, societal changes require adaptation, and this included
the closing of the Stanley as a movie theatre in 1990. It was put up
for sale in 1991 and came very close to becoming a gutted retail
space. Thankfully the Stanley Theatre Society, along with provincial government funding, came to the rescue, and the Stanley got a
much-needed renovation and a new life as a live theatre venue.

The stories about the Stanley are varied, but I was lucky enough
to talk with someone who went there specifically to seek the paranormal. As it turns out, the theatre community embraces this.

Gina Vancek of HauntedHistoryBC.com (who lives in her own
haunted condominium) attended a fundraiser for the theatre with
her sister and husband, put on by the people at the Ghostly Walking
Tours and Vancouver Cornerstone Paranormal. This fundraiser was
essentially a demonstration of different paranormal techniques and
research methods, as well as the sharing of some fun paranormal
anecdotes and stories.

The Stanley seats 650 people, but the event had been capped at
50 people. They had reserved the theatre for their group alone, so
it was an intimate gathering in a large space. They all got a tour of
the theatre and were told stories, and then they were broken up into
smaller groups.

Gina's group began upstairs in the mezzanine, on the far left, facing the stage, where it was soon discovered that there were distinctly cold spots. Using an EMF meter—an instrument that measures electromagnetic frequency and translates it into metered lights that go from green to yellow to red to show the intensity—the demonstrators pointed it at the cold spot in the mezzanine, and the meter went off right away.

The group moved on to the next demonstration, opposite the mezzanine level, on the far right of the stage, where demonstrators used an SLS (structured light sensor) camera, which measures different points of light to create a picture using stick figures. In that area, the SLS camera showed stick figures, which corroborated with reports of those who had seen shadow figures, sensed movement, and felt like they weren't alone, even if to the naked eye nobody else was around.

The group then moved to the control booth, where a lot of paranormal activity had been reported; there the group members tried digital recorders to see if they could capture EVPs (electronic voice phenomena). While not successful at catching anything on the recorders, all three of the people in the group experienced multiple sightings out of the corner of their eye (this is known as "corner of the eye phenomena" or COTEP) and were quite shocked at how much all three of them saw, yet didn't quite see.

Upstairs in the lobby, behind the stage, a ghost box was set up. This technology sweeps through radio bands and allows spirits to choose words with which to communicate out of the static. While Gina, her husband, and her sister Victoria did not have any luck using the ghost box, other groups that came through did. Contact was made with at least one spirit interested in communicating.

Psychic readings were offered at the next station, which was located in the women's dressing room. Kathryn, the medium there, channelled a female spirit in the room; she felt that the energy that was coming through was that of the spirit of an employee of the theatre or an actress who had performed there.

The reading Kathryn did for Gina's husband was quite shocking for all of them as Kathryn began speaking truths she could not have otherwise known. Then she told Gina details about a recent business transaction and where she would be able to live in the future, all things that Gina had been dealing with. When it was Victoria's turn for a reading, she was told she had some intuitive gifts and that the spirit of a younger man was sometimes around her. Kathryn related the circumstances of this young man's death: he was a relative, and the details of his passing as Kathryn described them were accurate.

Once all the different groups had progressed through all the stations, they gathered together again and told some ghost stories, including one of a production that had been performed. From the mezzanine level, some of the actors on stage saw a woman jump from the mezzanine level to the main floor of the theatre below. She appeared so real, and enough people saw her, that the play was halted while staff members checked the area—but no one was found.

Even today, while in the middle of the play, actors will see people who are not really there; sometimes these ghostly audience members show up for dress rehearsals too. The only sign they are not genuinely alive is that they appear on closer inspection to be slightly transparent.

The Stanley also seems to have a plumbing problem—well, not quite, but it does involve water. People working alone in the theatre have frequently reported the sound of running water. When they go to check the source of the noise, they discover that the taps have been turned on by unknown means—no explanation, just water rushing down the drain.

THE VOGUE

HE VOGUE THEATRE, DESIGNED TO BE A MOVIE THEATRE
when it came into being in 1941, has a few entities that appear
to have made this building their home. One is a dark-haired
man who appears throughout the premises.

Meghan (not her real name) worked as an usher at the theatre for
a time and vividly recalls seeing the dark-haired man; it was her onc
and only experience seeing a ghost.

"It was just before we opened the doors to the public," she says.
"They were still locked. I had come around the corner and was
heading to the lobby, and standing ahead of me was a man with dark
hair. I spoke to him, thinking perhaps he'd got in somehow; I knew he
wasn't a staff member. I said, 'Excuse me, sir, we're not quite ready to
have you in the theatre just yet.' He turned and looked at me—and
then I knew that what I was seeing was not normal because I could
see through him just a bit.

"He looked at me with no expression on his face and just sort of
faded away. I went and found my friend, also an usher, and told her
what had happened. She told me she'd seen him before too, but she
had figured she was imagining it.

"Turns out he'd been spotted all over—the lobby, the theatre
itself, the stage, the projection booth. If you wanted to avoid him,
it wasn't going to happen; you were guaranteed to run into him. I
wasn't overly freaked out, but I was definitely not as comfortable in
the theatre as I'd been before that happened."

This was not the first time this dark-haired figure had shown
himself to individuals. People reported seeing him in the theatre and

then seeing him dissolve once spotted; others heard noises in places where there shouldn't have been; still others had a stomach-clenching feeling of being watched, knowing they were no longer alone in the room even though it appeared they were. People have also felt drops in temperature and the feeling of being brushed past.

Staff have also experienced an entity that sometimes moves angrily through the basement corridor, making banging noises and slamming doors in the rooms below. (If I were the night guard, I would not stay long once I'd had *that* little experience in an empty theatre!) And sometimes, in the projection room, the odour of cigars and alcohol can be smelled when no one has been in there.

The common theory is that the entity was a deceased staff member, perhaps a manager who was responsible for keeping the theatre running. It would explain why he's seen all over the theatre.

A place does not require a death to have occurred onsite to be haunted. For many people, the attachment is strong enough that their energy wants to return; for some, they have no idea they're dead and are simply reporting to work as normal. I can't imagine how frustrating it would be to be the manager of a business, to not realize you were dead, but find that everything you wanted done was either ignored or done entirely differently. No wonder this particular ghost gets annoyed sometimes.

THE ORPHEUM

THE ORPHEUM THEATRE OPENED IN 1927 AND COST $1.25 million to build—the equivalent of over $18 million in 2021. It was built to be a vaudeville theatre and appears to have been very successful. When the popularity of vaudeville waned, the theatre scrambled to find a new purpose.

While it would host the occasional live performance, for many years it mostly functioned as a movie theatre. It came very close to being gutted and turned into a multiplex in 1973, but a community movement saved the Orpheum; it went on to be fully restored and is now the stunning theatre it is today. Home to the Vancouver Symphony Orchestra, it has also appeared in a number of movies and television shows, sought out for its beauty and the calibre of its restoration.

Three ghosts are most frequently spotted there.

Back in the day, men's bathrooms commonly had attendants; it seems one of the theatre's ghosts who is spotted down there on a semi-regular basis believes this is a custom that should continue. The only time he gets scary is if a woman goes in there for whatever reason. This is understandable as it was probably one of his primary jobs to make sure that all went smoothly in his porcelain kingdom. That would not be the case if his area was invaded by women.

Cheryl, one of the cleaners at the Orpheum, had the unpleasant task of having to clean the downstairs bathrooms. The women's bathroom went smoothly enough, but Cheryl says the minute she crossed the threshold into the men's bathroom she felt like she was being yelled at by a voice she couldn't hear. It was almost as if she'd walked into a world of anger. Cheryl had not heard any of the ghost stories of the theatre and was caught completely off guard by this experience. So she made a deal with her boss: he would clean the men's bathroom while she would do the rest of the lower level. Cheryl never set foot in that room again.

There's also the spirit of a woman in the audience area of the main part of the theatre. She's very enthusiastic with her praise and is seen standing up and applauding, but there is no way to charge her for the huge number of performances she's been spotted at. Always appearing in the same outdated outfit, with an old-fashioned hairstyle and a barely perceptible glow around her, she seems to be invisible to the audience, but those on stage and those accustomed to her presence know exactly where to look.

It's suspected that the original departed staff may have some representatives sticking around. Folding seats go down by themselves, footsteps have been heard in the main auditorium when it is empty, and doors have opened and closed on their own accord as if someone is entering or exiting the theatre. People have also felt someone pass in the rows behind them, only to turn and look to see no one there.

One of the sadder stories is that of the ghost of a performer still trapped onstage. The gentleman was an acrobat in a vaudeville performance, and he fell and died. He's seen now as a ball of light that moves with purpose around the stage; others have seen him as a man standing on the edge of the stage, looking out sadly. Is he stuck in place? Can he leave the stage if he wants to? Is he aware he had an accident? I hope he still gets some small joy in continuing to perform.

I BELIEVE THAT because of all the activity that takes place within theatres—the drama, the creativity, the magic shared between performers and their audience—they will always be profoundly haunted. So, the next time you're at a play or concert in an old theatre, see if you can intuit anything unusual. It can be difficult to do in a place full of other living people and their energy, but now and then, if you find yourself in a theatre lobby or bathroom without anyone else around, you may get the sense that you're not alone at all.

FAIRACRES MANSION:
BURNABY ART GALLERY

AIRACRES MANSION IS A PRIVATE HOME BUILT BY WEALTHY people, which sounds pretty typical for those who can afford it. But what isn't so typical is that Fairacres, also known as Ceperley House, has some fantastic twists and turns in its history.

Grace Ceperley and her husband Henry built the spectacular mansion, beginning in 1910 and finishing in 1911. Grace's money—inherited from Arthur Ferguson, a relative and Vancouver pioneer—financed the building of the lavish home on a twenty-acre estate on the banks of Deer Lake. The home was the most expensive in the region at the time, costing $150,000, which would come to just over $3.1 million today.

The architectural style was heavily influenced by the owners' British roots, and many of the details and fixtures, such as the tiles, were imported from England. The mansion was a sprawling masterpiece of the Arts and Crafts style that was so popular at the time. Not just the house was built but also several outbuildings, to service it. A chauffeur's cottage and garage as well as stables for the horses shows the transition between the old and new transportation methods that existed at that time. There was an aviary, gazebo, pergola, gardeners' cottage, and a steam plant to provide the house with heat and hot water.

Grace and Henry's dream home was by all accounts a happy one. Grace adored gardening; indeed, half the estate was made up of gardens. Grace also enjoyed the peace and quiet that her rural

paradise provided, and so it was a shame that she was only able to enjoy it for seven years; she died quite young at the age of fifty-four.

In her will, Grace left the home to her husband with the stipulation that if it was ever sold, money would be given to Stanley Park to create a play park for children. Henry did sell the house in 1919 and went to the States, but the park was not built until after Henry died in 1929. Some say this is the reason Grace never left her beloved home, even after she died. And it appears she is not the mansion's only spectral resident.

The house then went on a bit of a crazy ride in terms of ownership and utilization. After Henry sold the home, it passed through a series of private owners until it was used by the City of Vancouver as a temporary tuberculosis asylum while that terrible disease was brought under control. It then became an abbey for an order of Benedictine monks who stayed from 1939 till 1954, when they built their own abbey and departed the mansion.

In the mid-1950s, a cult called the Temple of More Abundant Life moved in and used it as their headquarters, living quarters, and school. It was later revealed that their founder and leader, a man by the name of William Franklin Wolsey, was wanted on a string of charges in the US; unsurprisingly, the cult was exposed as a source of bigamy, incest, abuse of children, and other horrible acts. In light of Grace's affinity for children, this was an affront to all she was known to have held dear. And so when Wolsey's despicable nature became public knowledge, he slithered away and left the mansion behind.

The building's next incarnation was as a frat house, leased by students from Simon Fraser University. However, this arrangement did not last long as the paranormal events did not lend themselves well to restful nights or focusing on grades. The young men were bothered by noises and banging, and a couple of them were scared enough to admit to seeing an older, spectral woman who was very disapproving of their lifestyle choices. Usually they would admit this as they were moving out, or they would tell the tales only after they had already left.

By 1966 the City of Burnaby had bought the building; its goal was to preserve Fairacres by turning it into an art gallery, but naturally renovations were needed. After its use by so many different groups for so many years, the plan was to restore Fairacres to its original glory—but if there's one thing ghosts seem to get upset about, it's renovations. Stories of the paranormal that had never really been all that mainstream, even from the frat members, suddenly became commonplace. There was talk of a woman in white who was often seen walking throughout the main floor, and an older gentleman dressed in old-fashioned clothing was often seen ascending and descending the stairs. Workers would frequently realize their tools were missing, and the people in charge of the renovation couldn't get contractors to complete the job without quitting halfway through.

One worker, whose office was on the second floor, continually heard footsteps and the sound of running, right above her head, on the uninhabited third floor. Others related stories of people going up to the third floor and seeing apparitions of children who ran away when spotted; this confirmed what the poor office worker was experiencing.

Resident ghosts include a young girl who cries softly; she's seen at the top of the stairs watching workers below. There are also faces of children seen in the third-floor windows, and a general atmosphere of sadness lingers in the area. The sounds of coughing or wheezing echo from certain areas on the second floor so clearly that people often go looking for the source, only to find themselves entirely alone or mistaken by someone else for making the coughing sounds. Some who have encountered Grace Ceperley herself have described her as serene, while other have said she seems grieved.

Visitors and staff alike have reported stories of noises, things being moved, the sound of footsteps, voices, and giggling—and, of course, apparitions spotted out of the corner of one's eye. Drops in temperature are also common, along with voices coming from nowhere. Loud banging occurs even when the building is empty.

Frank, who worked security for Fairacres and the art gallery, says that getting people to take on the Fairacres job is not easy. Multiple false alarms are triggered from the interior alarms, though no perimeter alarm has gone off; this means that the security guard has to go into the building and "clear" it—starting at the top floor and walking all the way through, checking every room and every floor. Most of the new people who take on the Fairacres security job only do it once, and then quit the company, not wanting to talk about why they left. Some simply refuse to ever return to Fairacres.

Who is it that lingers at Fairacres? It seems it may be a large group of spirits. Grace and her husband Henry seem to be frequent, if not resident, spirits; there are also the spirits of children from the time of the cult, the odd monk who passed away in the home, and the former patients of the tuberculosis asylum who never got to go home.

After wandering around Fairacres, I would say it's dripping in paranormal energy. However, after a walk around the remaining outbuildings as well as some of the outdoor gardens, I would conclude that it is primarily the house that has activity—it just seems to have a different energy moving through it, or perhaps resident in it. I have the impression that the outbuildings are visited frequently by a paranormal energy, perhaps from the house, but it's the house itself that is a real mess of energy. I visited just as the gallery was opening so I could get as "clean" a feeling as possible there, and I definitely sensed the presence of an older woman, and children as well. I think they're connected. Perhaps, though born decades apart, the energy of Grace is there to protect the children in a way they never were during the dark years of the cult. I think Grace still feels responsible for what happens in her home, and I don't think she'll be going anywhere soon.

If you're interested in paranormal activity, you'll get a lot out of wandering all through the former Fairacres estate; it's a powerful site in a powerful area. If you told me there are other ghost stories and paranormal reports around Deer Lake in general, I would not be surprised; Fairacres seems like a train station of energy, in a way, with plenty moving through, and often very busy. It's a gorgeous house on a spectacular property, and I'm so relieved to see it preserved and protected in the way it deserves. If you do get the chance to visit, please say hello to Grace for me.

A PRIVATE HOME ON
MARINE DRIVE

A POSITIVE PERSON WITH A SHY, QUICK SMILE, KRISTY GOT in touch after reading my first book, *Victoria's Most Haunted*, and was eager to share her story.

Her grandparents had immigrated to Canada from Mainland China in the 1950s and found financial success here after launching a number of businesses. They'd worked hard over the years and became very wealthy. Their house—a great, big eleven-bedroom on South West Marine Drive—represented their success, and Kristy's grandparents had no plans to give it up anytime soon.

Kristy visited her grandparents often when she was growing up; the family was close-knit, and parents and grandparents were respected and deferred to. If Kristy's mom got a call to come for dinner or a party, or any other reason Kristy's grandmother came up with, it wasn't a question of whether or not they would go—they simply went. This meant they were at the house frequently, around three or four times a week. The only problem was that Kristy hated the house.

She realized her grandparents' cultural bias was to shut down any stories that involved spirits or ghosts, so when she began to sense something unusual was going on, she thought she was going nuts. As a result, Kristy grew up feeling isolated and unheard. She didn't trust her instincts, and she fundamentally doubted herself as she continued to be terrorized by the place her grandparents called home.

Kristy's earliest memory of something strange going on took

place when she was six years old. The family would often stay over at her grandparents' house, especially on weekends or holidays, and on this occasion it was just another weekend sleepover. The family enjoyed being together, and it was a luxury for her mother to not have to worry about taking care of her own house and meals; as hostess, Kristy's grandmother took care of all that.

When it was bedtime, Kristy was to head upstairs to her room—she had her own room in this house—and so she began her trek up the grand staircase. But just as she began to climb the stairs, she stopped cold as she saw a shadow run past the top of the stairs and down the hallway, from left to right. Kristy had to get to the top of the stairs and go right—where the shadow had gone—and then the hallways branched off again to the left and right. As she got to the top of the stairs and turned right, she saw another shadow figure, or perhaps the same one, run across the doorway to the hallway that led to her room.

Though she had felt uncomfortable in the house for as long as she could remember, Kristy had never had anything happen like this. This went beyond mere feelings; now something was genuinely happening. She turned on her heel, fled back down the stairs as fast as she could, and burst back into the living room where her mother, father, and grandparents were talking.

She flung herself into her mother's arms, and her mother tried to get out of her what had scared her so badly as it was quite obvious she was terrified. As Kristy struggled to explain what she'd seen, her grandmother grew agitated and annoyed.

"Your child is lying and full of imagination," her grandmother snapped at Kristy's mother.

This cut Kristy to the core; not only did it hurt to be called a liar, she could not understand why anyone would lie about this. She was an obedient child—went to bed on time, ate her vegetables, was good in school. She always tried her best to please the adults in her life, so her grandmother's reaction was all the more upsetting.

Finally, after her mother got her calmed down, Kristy was able to explain what she'd seen and why it scared her so much. What was really terrifying her now was the prospect of going up to the bedroom alone. So her mother agreed to go with her, while her grandmother strongly advised against "indulging her imagination." As Kristy and her mom went upstairs, she held her mother's hand so tightly that her mother asked her to loosen up a little bit. They walked up the stairs, went along the hallway, and then headed to the left to go down toward Kristy's room.

They got all the way down the hallway and saw nothing out of the ordinary. Kristy's mom led her into the room, got her tucked in, turned out the lights, and said good night. It took a very long time for Kristy to fall asleep that night, but sleep eventually came, and in the morning the event didn't seem as bad or as serious as it had the night before. Kristy still felt uncomfortable in the house, but she assumed that the event was a one-off and decided not to worry about it. But the event was not the last she'd experience.

Kristy told me it was almost as if that shadow figure running across the hall seemed to open a figurative door to more experiences. Soon things began happening—not all the time, but enough that she knew that at least every couple of months something would occur. It was bad enough seeing the shadows dart around, letting her know they were there but never staying still long enough to see them. Now the activity was ramping up, getting more personal, getting a lot more terrifying.

At this point the shadow figures had been showing up on and off for a couple of years. There were still the creepy feelings, the unexplained cold spots she would walk through, mostly upstairs, and an almost constant sense of being watched. Now that she was a bit older it seemed the energy wanted to scare her more.

One summer afternoon, while everyone was out in the backyard enjoying the patio, Kristy ventured alone into her grandparents' house to use the bathroom. She'd tried to wait till someone else was coming in as well, but by now she really had to go and could wait no longer. She slipped down the hall on the main floor to one of the downstairs bathrooms, turned on the light, and shut and locked the door. Sitting there, doing what she had to do, she felt the small room get colder and colder—and then the light just snapped off. This would not have been so bad, but this bathroom did not have a window, so now poor Kristy was sitting in the pitch black. She could feel herself begin to panic, and at this point, at age eight, she didn't know what to do. She pulled up her pants, managed to find the lock in the dark, threw open the door, and ran back into the yard.

Knowing her grandmother's feelings on the subject, she did not say anything to her mother until later. But rather than ask any questions, Kristy's mother seemed anxious to play it down, to dismiss it. "Well, it's an old house," she said, "and sometimes the wiring isn't great."

Kristy knew exactly what she'd experienced, and it wasn't bad wiring.

As she grew older, she had many other encounters in the house. A few times she'd been in her room and been woken up in the middle of the night to the sound of her mother's voice softly calling her name in the hallway, "Kristy, Kristy, come here . . ."

But Kristy, knowing her mother would simply enter the room if she needed her, would pull the covers over her head and pretend the voices weren't there.

As the years went by, her parents and grandparents would sometimes leave Kristy alone in the house to do schoolwork while they did the weekly shopping. Kristy was sometimes able to convince her parents to let her stay home at her own house, but most often the answer was "You don't want to disappoint your grandparents by not coming." So, once again, she would be off to the house on Marine Drive.

These times alone were not conducive to focused study times.

Kristy would always do her work in the kitchen with her back to the wall so she could see everything coming and going. It didn't always work, however, as she was often distracted by things flitting across doorways or in the large pantry, or hearing people walking around upstairs and opening and closing doors. Kristy never went up there to see them as she never wanted to know exactly what was up there. She had learned to not even bring it up with either her parents or grandparents; no one else seemed affected by the energy in the house, so she suffered alone.

Until one afternoon, when she was in high school.

Kristy had a good friend named Chelsea. Chelsea was everything Kristy wanted to be. She was fearless, did what she wanted, said what she wanted, and was a lot of fun. The two girls connected despite their vastly different personalities and became best friends. So much so that if Chelsea was over at Kristy's and they were summoned to the grandparents' house, Chelsea would come too, even for overnight stays. Kristy felt so much better having someone else there—and not only did Chelsea offer moral support, but she also believed Kristy. Chelsea said that she too felt the house was creepy, but she wasn't sure why.

One Saturday afternoon, Kristy's parents and grandparents had gone out to do grocery shopping, and Kristy and Chelsea were left to do schoolwork in the kitchen. But now, for the first time ever, strange things began happening when someone else was around.

Chelsea looked over at Kristy and said, "I thought we were here by ourselves."

Kristy assured her that they were; there was no one else in the house.

"Then who," continued Chelsea, "is *that?*" She pointed toward the ceiling as the very clear sound of someone walking around, and a door opening and closing, could be heard upstairs.

Kristy explained that this was just another way the energy in the house liked to mess with her.

Chelsea's reaction was one of annoyed protectiveness: She jumped up, grabbed Kristy's hand, and said, "This stops now!"

The two girls ran upstairs to the place where they had just heard the footsteps, and then stopped. The footsteps started up again, but this time on the third floor. Chelsea dragged Kristy up there, and they stopped again. They heard a bedroom door open and close on the second floor, so they ran back down, heading for the door. No sooner had they got there than they heard the footsteps again on the third floor, so back up they went.

By this point Kristy was getting more and more freaked out as she felt like they shouldn't mess with whatever it was. The only way she had survived so long in the house was by pretending whatever it was didn't exist, but now they were actively chasing it.

Kristy begged Chelsea to just let it go, and reluctantly Chelsea agreed. Kristy went back downstairs to the kitchen where she could have her back against the wall, but Chelsea went to use the upstairs bathroom before she came back down. Kristy heard her go in and close the door, and she focused on her work. Then she heard the toilet flush, the sink run, and the door open, but then the door slammed shut.

"Kristy!" Chelsea shouted, so loud that it echoed downstairs. She sounded scared.

Kristy bolted upstairs and opened the bathroom door, and a very freaked-out Chelsea grabbed her in a hug.

"Did you see anything when you came up to the door?" she asked.

Kristy said she had not.

Chelsea explained that everything had proceeded normally until Chelsea went to open the door to the bathroom. She had been looking down, tucking in her shirt, and as she opened the door, she saw feet—specifically, dark brown men's Oxford shoes, and the bottom part of the legs in light brown pants, right in front of the door. She did *not* want to look any higher, so she slammed the door and yelled for her friend.

The girls agreed that pursuing this ghost and literally chasing him around the house may not have been the best idea.

As frightening as this experience was, in a weird way it brought some closure for Kristy. She and her friend had done the unthinkable: Not only had they acknowledged what the presence was, they had chased it, and other than a nasty scare nothing terrible had happened. It had been a shared experience with her best friend, and now Kristy felt seen and heard and believed, so she was able to put her fear of whatever it was away.

Things still happened in the house. She would still see shadows and hear odd things, but she never again felt terror in her heart as she had when she was a little girl. Kristy has never had any other paranormal experiences anywhere else, but she figures she has had more than her fair share.

Her grandparents still live in that house, although their time there is coming to an end. With them getting on in age, and with all of those stairs, they will need to sell soon. Kristy wonders if the energy will be glad that the house is sold or if it will miss having Kristy around. Either way, she says, when the house goes up for sale, one thing is for sure: *she's* not buying it.

THE VANCOUVER POLICE MUSEUM

THE VANCOUVER POLICE MUSEUM, ESTABLISHED IN 1986 FOR the force's centenary celebrations, houses and displays artifacts that give us a glimpse into the history of the police and the cases they worked on for over 125 years of Vancouver's history.

The museum is housed in the former Coroner's Court building. Designed in 1932 by city architect Arthur J. Bird, Coroner's Court was a place with morgue facilities, where autopsies and forensic testing could be done to investigate any death that was deemed unusual or criminal in some way.

This building has seen the outcome of many bizarre, violent, heartbreaking, random, and planned deaths, so it's not all that surprising that it has managed to hold on to some of the energy that passed through it over the years. It was even used as a hospital briefly after the Battle of Ballantyne Pier in 1935, which involved a strike that got ugly and resulted in many people being injured. Mostly, however, this temporary hospital was not a place of healing but a place of the dead, a place for them to tell their last story through the hands of the coroners and lab technicians who worked to find answers. Sometimes energy gets left behind in such environments, for various reasons, but I will concede that not everyone is going to agree on this point.

Museum volunteer Rob Murray had reason to question the concept of the residual paranormal energy of a place when he volunteered at the museum for approximately six months. His role was to assist in the digitization and organization of the records as well as the physical space. But the museum director at the time always insisted that there were no ghosts at the site. Apparently there had been other volunteers who had experienced things, but as is often the case, those in charge decided to take the official position that the museum was not haunted. (It would be nice if that made a difference to the ghosts.) They claimed that since this was a place where they solved crimes, there would be closure, so therefore no ghosts.

In my experience, people in management resort to outright denial for various reasons. One is personal conviction—essentially, they don't believe in "that sort of thing," so naturally there could be no ghosts, as they don't believe they exist. Another reason is that they're pretty sure there is something happening, but they don't want to scare away visitors or volunteers, so they claim there are no ghosts and let the visitors and staff figure it out—or at least decide for themselves. Or it's a simple matter of being terrified of the whole concept of ghosts, so they resort to denial to cope with or escape their fear. I must admit that I'm often most intrigued by those who choose firm non-belief based on personal conviction because, generally, they end up having the most profound paranormal experiences, such as a face-to-face encounters with the resident energy. I have seen many instances when those individuals are forever changed.

The museum was divided into three main areas: the third floor, open to the public, used by all, where the majority of the museum collection is housed and displayed. The second floor was the storage for the gift shop—generally off limits to the public, and the place where Rob was working the most on his own. The first floor—the basement, really—was where the morgue and autopsy rooms were; this is where the general hands-on practice of pathology would happen. There was even a blood-drying room.

In general, the second floor was most notorious for being the creepiest part of the building, as no one had any reason to go into the basement and gauge the creepiness factor there. Volunteers would generally run up to the second-floor storage to get what was required for the gift shop, but no one hung around there, and most left by running down the stairs, even though the reason for the hurry was never discussed.

In the basement there was more storage of different items, including old uniforms from long-passed officers, as well as some records and artifacts. There were also murder weapons, not on display but perhaps carrying their own dark energy. No one in the museum had much reason to go down there, and they didn't if they could avoid it.

The museum floor, the third floor, was never a problem; everything seemed relatively normal up there. But the second floor—previously a csi lab, now used for storage and Rob's work area—was different. Rob felt uneasy up there; he always had a vague sense of being watched or observed, even though it was now just a storage area. It was a very noisy building, with lots of creaks and bangs, though you could chalk that up to it being an old structure, but Rob says that at night the atmosphere changed—if anything, the building became louder, and that sense of being watched intensified. When he worked on digitizing after dark, he would try to avoid his uneasy feelings by putting his headphones on to block the sounds. But it didn't always work; sometimes the noises were just too loud.

One night, just after darkness had fallen, Rob's feeling of being watched was so intense that he felt like he was intruding on someone's personal space—as if he was in someone's way and they were not pleased to have him there. It was so strong that the feeling seemed to seep out of the walls. Rob lasted an extra half hour and then had to go; there was no way he was going to be able to concentrate on anything. As he left, he mentioned to the administrator, who was working on another floor, that he was thoroughly creeped out and

that he was leaving. The administrator was not surprised and agreed that it was a creepy place after dark.

Eventually, the reputation of the site inspired an investigation by Cornerstone Paranormal. While the findings were not shocking, they did provide some extra insight into the building itself. For example, in one formerly used area, where a receptionist would have sat, people had complained about feeling like someone was with them when they were alone. The investigators measured a significant cold spot in that area, and when they asked questions aloud, addressing any potential entities, the K2 meter (a device used to measure electrical energy and translate it into light patterns) responded to yes-or-no questions by increasing or decreasing the brightness of the device's lights. They also measured the cold area moving from left to right and hovering over the desk. Was this a former employee who, as far as they were concerned, was still employed at the Coroner's Court building?

The investigators also measured some K2 reactions in a closet in a side office, as if something was trying to hide from them. The closet had no wiring near it and was on an outside wall, so the meter was reading something that was not conventionally explainable. They also had reactions from the energy when questions were asked aloud, and the K2 meter lit up in response.

There is a secondary or overflow morgue in the building that was only used once, when the Second Narrows Bridge (renamed the Iron Workers Memorial Bridge) collapsed during construction in 1957, sending seventy-five workers almost thirty metres down into the water below. Nineteen workers died in the collapse, and the dead overwhelmed the regular morgues. Everyone felt a presence in this former secondary morgue. There was also a cold spot over the autopsy tables and some activity on the SLS camera.

Additionally, there were noises and activity in one of the laboratories that could not be attributed to anything physical, and an EVP was caught in the main morgue. (EVP stands for *electronic voice phenomena,* which refers to voices that can't be heard with your ears alone, but can be captured and heard in a digital recording.) This voice came in response to an investigator climbing into one of the body cabinets and lying down in the tray. The EVP told him to get out. If this was the energy of a former staff member, I'm sure they would not have found the sight of a living person climbing into the drawer for the dead very amusing or acceptable at all.

MY OWN TIME at the museum was admittedly unremarkable in terms of the paranormal. Is there energy there? Undoubtedly, but during opening hours and in the public spaces, that energy pulls back. But given Rob's account, I'm sure it would change after dark and in the private, forgotten places that fill this building.

As with most older buildings, the Vancouver Police Museum comes with a history, and given its origin story, it's not surprising it has an extra dose of energy. Add to that the residual energy of people seeking justice and solving crimes over the years, and its overall connection to grieving families, and it's reasonable to assume that the Vancouver Police Museum is haunted. All in all, it's a fascinating place to visit, and it provides an intriguing glimpse into Vancouver's past.

GASTOWN

G ASTOWN IS FULL OF THE PARANORMAL, WHICH IS UNSUR-
prising when one of the oldest sections of the city evolves into a
new, hip, and lively incarnation. Wherever you find a combination of historical locations and lots of people, you're likely to find
more reports of paranormal activity.

Easily one of the most historically charming areas in Vancouver,
with its Victorian buildings and cobblestone streets, Gastown
emerged from a single pub that opened in 1867. That particular
pub's owner, John "Gassy Jack" Deighton, was essentially the accidental founder of Gastown. With a sawmill and a port nearby, the
genesis of Vancouver quickly came about, and Gastown not only
became a place of business but also a place to party. Fishermen,
loggers, adventurers, prospectors, ships' captains and crews were all
there for different reasons at different times.

In the summer of 1886, most of the city's buildings were lost in
the Great Vancouver Fire, but they were rebuilt to be bigger and
better, and soon all the major shipping companies had docks in
Vancouver. Major merchants also established stores in Gastown,
including the Hudson's Bay Company, and there were still plenty of
grocery stores, bars, and other places to have a good time.

The 1930s marked a period of transition for Gastown. At one
point there were three hundred drinking establishments in a twelve-
block radius, and Gastown was reborn as a place of hard drinking,
hard living, and rowdy good times. After the Depression, it went
from being a busy, thriving hub to a neighbourhood in steep decline.
Not only was it becoming unattractive, but it was also downright

dangerous, and so Gastown went from being a vibrant, attractive centre to a problem area for city council to deal with.

By the 1960s, Gastown was in danger of being destroyed for the sake of a new highway that was slated to cut through the city. This was not unusual for the time but would surely have spelled disaster for any historic buildings in the city. Vancouver residents rallied and began putting pressure on governments to preserve these older, historically rich buildings, and they were successful—largely in part to the brave business people who established galleries, restaurants, and other interesting places for people to gather. Because of their foresight and commitment to history, these place-makers managed to turn Gastown around, and it has now become a popular tourist destination as well as a fun place for locals to have dinner or drinks. It's also one of the most haunted spaces in the city.

There are quite a few excellent walking ghost tours you can do in this part of the city, and I was lucky enough to meet with Lydia Williams who owns Ghostly Vancouver Tours. But I wasn't interested in seeing anything that had been covered before; I wanted to hear more about places that weren't that well known. For example, places like Blood Alley have already been heavily documented; Lydia, along with others who wish to remain anonymous, were a huge help in this regard.

This is not to say Blood Alley does not have its own story to tell. First of all, that's not even its official name; it's actually called Trounce Alley. The cobblestoned square was named Blood Alley Square by the city, in an attempt to create cachet for the public and to promote the story that Blood Alley was a place filled with blood because of local abattoirs (there weren't any) and that hangings took place here (they didn't). It was merely a clever marketing move that appears to have been successful.

Suffice it to say Blood Alley seems to be a connecting point for spirits, and it has been said that it may be a place of cross-over for ghostly energy. While we will make a few stops in Gastown, two places in particular—the Irish Heather and Shebeen—lead off of Blood Alley, and they have stories of their own to tell.

THE IRISH HEATHER

HE IRISH HEATHER GASTROPUB OPENED IN 1997 AND HAS transformed over the years to become a high-end restaurant. When they first moved into the space, the owners knew something was going on that was deeply paranormal. The building has an upper floor, and while it was unoccupied, the Irish Heather's owners would constantly hear footsteps above them, day and night. It didn't seem to matter when—something or someone would walk around upstairs at all hours. The owners also witnessed a rare, full-bodied apparition crossing at the back of the bar, not something you forget easily.

One of the servers told me that while it was unnerving at first, the presence now just feels like part of the place, like a sticky fridge door or a fussy beer tap; you learn about it and adapt. She has never seen anything, but she has heard footsteps upstairs just before opening and after closing. She has also been alone in the restaurant while feeling like she was not alone, but it has never made her feel unsafe or scared; she now sees it as a bonus that even when she is alone in the restaurant, she's never really alone. I think this is a great attitude.

When I stopped in to see what I could feel in this space it was pretty crowded. Why would this matter? It's hard to describe. Imagine you go into a room and there is only one other person in there. You can see them, you can describe them, and you will likely communicate with them. However, if you walk into the same room and there are a hundred people in there, and you have no idea who you are looking for, good luck trying to figure out anything about them. Essentially, the more energy there is in a room (we all have our own energy), the harder it is to pick up on any type of energy that no longer has a living body attached.

In any case, the Irish Heather is a beautiful place, and I have no doubt it has its own ghostly residents, but in crowded conditions I am not sensitive enough to be able to pick up on whether or not they are there—or where exactly they are.

SHEBEEN

S HEBEEN COULD BE CALLED A SISTER RESTAURANT TO THE Irish Heather; it is in fact owned by the same group of restaurants. Haunted buildings must not bother these owners, though, as this one seems to be even more haunted. It's situated just off Blood Alley and is an Irish whiskey tasting house, with tapas and charcuterie boards—pretty much the perfect restaurant as far as I'm concerned.

· This restaurant is one of the most actively haunted places in Gastown, and once again, the owners embrace it. There has been a ghost investigation here, put on by Paul Busch and the rest of the group from Cornerstone Paranormal. While they had a full-spectrum camera trained on the end of the bar, a full-sized apparition appeared on camera and then disappeared back behind the bar. The group was shocked.

When visiting a potentially haunted establishment, I always like to make a point of speaking to a server to get their impression of their workplace. The server here—let's call him Mike—said that while he knows the place is haunted he's never had anything too scary happen. He did once see a spoon fly off the bar before the place was open one day, and there was no one near it. It *flew*, he emphasized, it didn't just fall off the bar. Mike said that was certainly startling, but like the server at their sister restaurant, he figures it's just part of doing business in the old buildings of Gastown. While Mike is pretty laid back about the whole thing, he does know of people who have started work at Shebeen and then quit soon after; the atmosphere and activity were just too much for them.

KIMPRINTS

KIMPRINTS HAS TWO LOCATIONS: GASTOWN AND ENGLISH Bay. This particular haunting takes place in their Gastown store. They have been in this location since 1984, offering custom framing, original art, and art supplies.

They have a lot of activity going on in the basement—noises, rustling, footsteps. At one ghost investigation by Cornerstone Paranormal, K2 meters were set up in the corner. These meters are usually handheld with a set of lights that measure electromagnetic energy. Sometimes things like unprotected wires can cause false readings, but most experienced investigators will check out an area ahead of time to ensure they're not picking up any other type of energy. Down in the basement of Kimprints, the K2 meter had been set up beside the custom framing cutting board, and the meter started going off the charts—something was triggering all the lights to turn on repeatedly. Sometimes a K2 meter can be used as a way to communicate with energy by asking questions and watching the lights for a response, but this time, the lights simply kept flickering to the maximum level, on and off. The meter had been set up in the part of the basement where the staff had said they felt something like a presence. Another odd bit of activity in the basement was the sound of a dog barking. There were no dogs anywhere in the building, but a dog barking could be clearly heard from below.

In the upstairs of the building there's a shadow that the living must contend with, in the upper level of the main store. The shadow seems to appear and disappear at will, and while not specifically looking to be noticed, its presence is always observed.

ALIBI ROOM

T HE ALIBI ROOM, A "MODERN TAVERN," IS THE CURRENT
resident at an address with a long history. Constructed in
1913, this old building has housed a number of businesses. Its
location, close to the port of Vancouver as well as the rail line, made
it an ideal spot for early business owners in the fur trade and glove
manufacturing. It eventually became a restaurant and watering hole
in the 1970s, when it was known as the Banjo Room. There were
more iterations of restaurants and lounges after that until the Alibi
Room came into being in 1998 and was reestablished in 2006. It's
been going strong ever since; with over fifty beers on tap, it's easy to
figure out why.

With its brick interior, most of its original architectural features
intact, and gorgeous, large windows, the building has been used as
a filming location many times; anyone can see why location scouts
would be drawn to it. However, they often get more than they
bargain for.

On one particular movie shoot, the director gave the standard
call for quiet on the set, and all attendees (at least those who were
living) stopped what they were doing and went silent. And yet the
sound of footsteps were heard. Production assistants checked on
the source, but they came back with nothing to report, and by this
point the sound of the footsteps had stopped.

"Quiet on set!" the director called out again. And then there were
more footsteps.

This happened a few more times, but eventually the director,
cast, and crew were able to get in their take when the footsteps

finally faded away. Their source must have eventually reached their unknown destination.

The washrooms also seem to be points of activity of the paranormal kind. In the women's washroom, shadow figures can be seen moving around, and sometimes staff have reported feeling uneasy in there. And during a king tide (an exceptionally high tide) ocean water sometimes seeps into the men's washroom; perhaps the presence of the salt water, which is known to trap energies, has an effect on the building.

But most of the ghostly activity occurs in the basement. Down there, in the kitchen area, a dishwasher named Aaron was the most effected by the presence that seemed to make this spot home.

The presence in the basement is seen as a shadow and is felt as a negative force, bringing sad, energy-draining feelings that have a profound effect on one's mood. The dish room there is separate from the rest of the restaurant, so dishwashing is an isolating job. Not a great set-up if you're being visited by an energy-draining entity that brings sadness.

Aaron, at a loss for how to deal with the situation, decided it couldn't get any worse if he took action. So he spoke out loud the next time the spirit was in the room. He acknowledged it and said he was sorry it was feeling so bad, but asserted that while he was aware of its feelings, he didn't want to share them. The entity faded, but when it came back again, as it seemed to every time Aaron was working, Aaron would begin to sing. This seemed to change everything. The room felt lighter and happier, so Aaron kept up the practice. Whenever the energy would show up in his workspace, Aaron would start singing, and the atmosphere would immediately shift to one of positivity. Aaron figures it made the mood and the energy much more positive for both of them, and he was relieved he could do something to change the situation.

GASTOWN HAS SO much history and so much interesting energy, and it's definitely worth checking out. If you have the time, go on one of the Ghostly Vancouver Tours that are offered there; you'll not only learn about the energy that lingers in the area, but you'll also gain a deeper understanding of its rich history and how Gastown became the place it is today, with its brewpubs, movie locations, ghosts, and more.

GALBRAITH HOUSE

N EW WESTMINSTER IS THE OLDEST PART OF VANCOUVER, SO
it's not a huge surprise that it's the home of a few ghost stories.
In the early days of colonized Canada, many intrepid families
were drawn from their homelands to explore the possibilities that lay
on the west coast. Their tenacious spirits live on today—sometimes
in more ways than one.

The Galbraith family—Hugh, his wife Jane, and their eight
children—were Scottish settlers who moved to New Westminster
from New Brunswick in 1884. Hugh had made his money as a lumber
baron and had set up a millwork business to produce beautifully
crafted wooden items and finishes for other wealthy people who were
building masterpiece homes. When he and his family moved to New
Westminster, Hugh was already in his fifties, but that didn't stop him
from doing what was expected of him as a Scottish immigrant: build
a big house. The family built their Queen Anne Revival-style home
in the Brow of the Hill area, a prestigious location at the time. The
two-and-a-half-storey house overlooked the burgeoning city and had
a view of the Fraser River, which was a growing source of income.

Galbraith House was built circa 1892 and was, by all accounts,
well loved by the whole family. They used the house to showcase
the craftsmanship and high quality of the items produced in their
workshop, and the home remained part of the family's life until the
1940s. The family business had burned to the ground in 1932, and
with no means of income (the 1930s were not an ideal time to revive
a business) and mounting unpaid taxes, it was only a matter of time
before the family had to sell their beloved home.

The house then went through the typical pattern of decline as these stately old homes so often seem to do. It became headquarters for the local Soroptimist Club and subsequently a hostel for military personnel during the Second World War, and was then converted into a rooming house before being bought and sold a few times, eventually getting a much-needed renovation in 2004; since then, it has been used to house offices. Through all of these changes, one thing seems to have remained the same: Hugh Galbraith has never left the house that he built at the pinnacle of his success for his family and as a showpiece to display to the world.

From the mid-1990s to the early 2000s, the house was home to the BCCPA (British Columbia Crime Prevention Association), an organization that works in partnership with police agencies throughout BC. Since it was the headquarters for the organization, many people worked there, and people from all over BC went there for meetings on various province-wide projects and initiatives.

The house was already known for paranormal events; unexplained activity was a daily occurrence—doors closing on their own, the sound of children laughing and running around on the upper level, items flying off shelves, footsteps when no one was there or the building was otherwise empty. More than once a middle-aged man in period clothing was seen quietly standing in the corner of the great room, the former ballroom.

The house was set up to accommodate offices while preserving much of its original charm. On the main floor was a parlour, a dining room, a kitchen, and what was once a ballroom, all turned into offices, as were the rooms on the second floor where previously there had been bedrooms. The third level was probably servants' quarters, as they were reached by ascending a hidden back staircase; it was now used as a small apartment for people visiting from out of town. The basement, with its concrete floors, was below grade, with small windows perched high but covered by bushes outside.

Tani, whose haunted-apartment story readers may recall from *Victoria's Most Haunted*, was working at Galbraith House for the BCCPA, and while she knew the house had a reputation, she was not quite prepared for how real it all would become. She says, "I had an office at Galbraith House and travelled there several times a month. Many times, when I had meetings over two or more days, I would stay at a hotel that was walking distance from the offices. Even though there was a small apartment-type area on the very top floor where members of the BCCPA could stay, no one ever did—certainly not me.

"Fifteen years ago, a colleague from Kelowna was at Galbraith House for meetings held over two days, as was I. At the end of the first day, when I was leaving the office, heading to the hotel for the night, I asked my colleague if he was staying at the same hotel. He indicated he had opted to make use of the upstairs apartment for the night. I looked at him like he was nuts and told him there was way too much creepy stuff happening up there, and that was why I always stayed at the hotel. He scoffed, saying he did not believe in such things and that he would come to the hotel the following morning to join me in the restaurant for breakfast prior to the meeting.

"The next morning I called his cell phone, and he said he was already downstairs in the dining room. I was a little surprised as it was quite early and I did not expect to see him for another hour or so. I made my way to the dining room, where I saw him seated at a table. With one look at him, I knew something was up. He looked very tired, tousled, and a little cranky. I asked him if he was feeling all right, and if he slept well. He looked at me, leaned across the table, and said, 'I checked into the hotel at 2:00 AM. Shit was going on last night and I couldn't stay there. And if you tell anybody, I will totally deny this conversation.' I was confused, so I asked him what had happened and why he had come to the hotel so late at night.

"He said that he locked up the house—he was the only one there—and went to bed upstairs in the suite. At about midnight, he started hearing odd banging noises and unusual sounds. Then there were footsteps. He thought for sure that it was another colleague who had keys to the house, and that they had snuck in and were trying to scare him. My friend thought he would catch this guy at his own game and was trying to turn the tables to give *him* a good scare. So he snuck down the hidden back stairs to surprise the other guy. But every time he went down, he would hear the footsteps upstairs, and every time he went up, he would hear them downstairs.

"After a while, it dawned on him that he was truly alone in the house, and that the footsteps he was hearing were not of the living kind. Once he realized there was no other person in the house, he could not get out of there fast enough. The fact that he had been creepily stealthing around in his underwear while carrying a piece of wood did not add to his personal pride level. I looked him straight in his embarrassed face and said, 'I told you so!'

"The BCCPA relied heavily on government support, and as a show of appreciation they hosted a garden party of sorts for the solicitor general at the time. It was also an open house, showcasing to the public the organization's work and contributions to crime prevention in the community.

"The party was scheduled to start at 2:00 PM, so in the morning, members of the organization and several volunteers rushed about to get everything ready. There were chairs and tables to set up, speakers and microphones to check, and lots of food and drink to prepare.

"The kitchen at Galbraith was enormous—very much in the original state but updated with modern appliances, with the original cupboards and intricate woodwork still intact. The ceiling was very high, at least twelve feet. The upper cupboards were very tall, but they did not meet the ceiling.

"There was a space between the top of the cupboards and the ceiling that held a lot of vintage tins, the kind you'd imagine being at Oleson's Mercantile on *Little House on the Prairie*. These tins, although once used, were now strictly for décor and were set back against the wall. I was standing at the counter with a volunteer, arranging sandwiches on a platter, when I felt something brush past me; this was instantly followed by a very loud crash at my feet. Startled, I looked down to see one of the tins from above on the floor, and the lid several feet away. I looked at the lady standing next to me; her face was sheet white and her eyes were as wide as saucers. 'Holy smokes,' I said, 'where did *that* come from?' She pointed upwards and said, 'Up there.' I later told one of my colleagues what had happened, and they said, 'Yes, Hugh does not like it when there are a lot of people at his house. He has been known to throw things.'

"Another time, just before Christmas, a couple of older volunteers were at the house on a Saturday, decorating the Christmas tree in the great room (the former ballroom). One of the ladies left the room to get another box of decorations from downstairs. As she was walking back up, she heard the other lady talking to someone. When she entered the great room, there was no one there but the other lady. 'Did I hear you talking to someone?' the first lady asked. The second lady replied that she had turned around and saw an older gentleman standing in the corner watching her decorate. She asked him if he was there to assist, but he did not reply. When she turned to see the first lady enter the room, he was gone. She had said he was dressed rather oddly, and was wearing an older style black hat. The other lady, aware that Mr. Galbraith sometimes made an appearance, directed the first lady to a photo of the Galbraith family that was hanging in the hall. 'That is the man that was just here!' she said. The man in the picture she was pointing to was Hugh Galbraith.

"By far the most unsettling part of the house was the basement; it used to be a recreation centre for soldiers in the Second World War who were training before being deployed. They had even painted a mural on the wall of what was the billiard room, and it still exists to this day. In this mural, lovely saloon-type girls continue to dance in the gloom of what was once a place of fun and relaxation. The area where the mural is was turned into a small meeting room, and the rest of the basement was used mainly for storage. The energy down there was very heavy and quite dark. You never felt entirely by yourself down there, and it was quite different from the rest of the house, feelings-wise. It was a creepy place to go, and one would be very quick to find what they needed and more often than not bound back up two stairs at a time.

"There were many other strange incidents that occurred with some regularity at Galbraith House—doors opening and closing by themselves, strange noises, items being moved or falling off shelves. The clump of heavy boots going up or down stairs. One could literally feel a heaviness throughout the residence, and often a chill when entering certain rooms.

"I was in a board meeting in the great room one morning, and we all could hear a child laughing and running around upstairs. There was no one else in the house except those of us in the meeting, and there were definitely no children. Not surprisingly, no one wanted to check as no one had gone up there and there were certainly no children upstairs. The other reason no one bothered to check was that it was just an accepted thing that 'this happened,' and everyone knew it. There was no need to go up to check.

"I can unreservedly say with absolute conviction, through my own personal experiences, that Galbraith House is most definitely haunted by more than one spirit, and it is still home to the ghost of Hugh Galbraith."

The feeling I got when stopping by Galbraith House was not one of menace or evil, but that of an occupied home. A house that has the ghosts of its former residents in it doesn't have to be a bad or scary thing—depending on your fear threshold, I suppose. In any case, my intuition told me strongly that there was far more to Galbraith House than could be seen at first glance, and there was certainly more of the unseen that one could sense.

THE GULF OF GEORGIA CANNERY

YOU DON'T OFTEN HEAR OF FISH CANNERIES BEING haunted, but then again you don't often have a cannery that has been around as long as this one. The Gulf of Georgia Cannery in Steveston, a part of Richmond, is a national historic site, and with good reason. At one point in British Columbia history, canned salmon was among our largest and most lucrative exports.

In 1894, the cannery was constructed as a single production row for canning the fish that the Musqueam people had relied upon for generations. This was a very lucrative but labour-intensive operation, so every year the area would fill with migrant workers.

By the 1930s, technology caught up with the canning industry, and fast, efficient, modern machines took over many of the jobs previously held by workers. At this time, the major fish packing companies merged and became one larger conglomerate, leaving the Gulf of Georgia Cannery to quietly fall into retirement—but the Second World War quickly changed that. Herring was the new fish to find its way into the cannery's efficient system, and now there were countless employees making case after case of herring packed in tomato sauce, a vital source of protein for soldiers fighting overseas. It was the perfect food, cheap and full of good, healthy fats. Best of all, if the fish was a tiny bit past its prime, the tomato sauce covered that up.

The plant was busy all through the war years. However, once the war was over, so was the demand for cheap fish. People wanted to indulge in post-war modern luxury, and no one wanted to be reminded of shortages that had been brought on by the war. So the cannery switched gears once again.

The demand for herring reduction saved the plant. Essentially, this was the reduction of the fish into powder to be used as fertilizer of food for animals, and herring oil, which was very popular for its high levels of Omega 3 and the generally positive health benefits it offered. During this time, the cannery went through three expansions to accommodate the level of processing required to keep up with the massive amount of fish coming through its doors. However, as we humans are wont to do, we showed zero self-control, and the herring industry collapsed due to massive overfishing; workers pulled them out of the water faster than they could breed. By the 1960s, everything had slowed down again as the river became a trickle of fish that were still being processed. Eventually there was just not enough supply to keep the cannery open, and in 1979 the very last product left the cannery.

For the next few years the building was used as storage until it was transferred over to Parks Canada, and in 1994 it opened to the public. Today it's run by a non-profit organization, but is overseen by the federal government. All of these changes, regardless of owner-ship, use, or even the passage of time, do not seem to have hampered the presence of residual energy that is still in the Gulf of Georgia Cannery today.

There have been a few ghost investigations in the cannery, and I can tell you as someone with a finely honed sense for these things, I wholeheartedly agree with anyone who says the cannery is haunted.

The cannery staff have commented on the noises they hear coming from all around the museum when they know there is no one else there. Many times, they hear murmuring as if someone is having a low, private conversation, and they can't quite make out what is being said. One staff member recalls hearing a very raucous woman's laugh ring out while she was there on her own and the doors were all locked. She left early that day.

Visitors have mentioned feeling like there's more than just the living in the building, and staff are quick to reassure them that while they may feel other entities they've never been harmful or posed any threat to anyone.

Many paranormal investigation groups find the cannery to be consistently active, and a number of groups have done more than one investigation there. They have never been disappointed. Glen Ferguson from the Canadian Paranormal Society spent most of his investigation at the boat house (which is connected to the cannery), but one investigator was shocked by seeing a full-body apparition in the theatre area, as he had never seen one before. Another investigator heard voices coming through the spirit box, a piece of equipment that runs through all the bands of AM and FM radio and allows the spirits to pick out words with which to communicate or answer questions. Still another investigator was getting a lot of EVPs (electronic voice phenomenon) in real time. Most often ghosts have voices that we can't hear with our ears alone, but they can sometimes be captured using a digital voice recorder. In this instance, the investigators would ask a question, hold up the voice recorder for a few seconds, and then switch it off; then they would rewind it and play it back to hear if there was a response. They got immediate and intelligent responses to their questions.

Another group performed an all-night investigation involving various technology and cameras. It was their lucky night: Before they could even get the cameras set up, a full-bodied apparition—a man in overalls, an old hat, and boots—appeared so closely and clearly to the group that they decided to call it a night before the night had properly begun.

If you get out to Steveston, do check out the cannery. If you're looking to feel something paranormal, you won't be disappointed—and if you're looking to *see* something paranormal, well, you might just get your wish granted.

MESCALERO RESTAURANT AND MAXINE'S BEAUTY SCHOOL

M ESCALERO, FORMERLY LOCATED ON THE CORNER OF Bidwell and Davie, was a very popular Mediterranean-style restaurant in the West End of Vancouver. At least it was when pastry chef Rachel worked there. Alone. In the basement.

The building was originally constructed in the 1920s and housed Maxine's Beauty School and Boarding House. Rumour had it that this was a cover for a discreet brothel frequented by members of the Mob and the rich and philandering. It may have had a hand in rum running during British Columbia's brief experience with prohibition.

Another rumour that turned out to be true was that there were secret tunnels under the building; one went to a bathing house on English Bay beach (sounds like a perfect rum-running spot to me) and the other went to Gabriola Mansion, an infamous house known for its wealth, parties, and all sorts of dodgy shenanigans.

As one would expect, the beauty school was quite busy, and not just with women learning how to do hair. In fact, it would appear that most of the students had very little to do with learning beauty techniques and far more with making gentlemen visitors happy.

Maxine's eventually went out of business and was shut down, and after the building underwent a massive refurbishment, it was the perfect place to open a Spanish-inspired restaurant as the building itself looked like a small Spanish monastery.

People had spoken of the building being haunted by a few spirits, suspected to be former employees of Maxine's. Patrons of the restaurant commented that apparitions of young women could be spotted from time to time. There was the sad story of the young woman who'd been murdered just outside where the women's bathrooms were in the restaurant. People spoke of feeling sad or even frightened there. However, seeing a woman going in and out of the bathroom would not have raised many eyebrows, so people often didn't realize what they were seeing.

Rachel, the pastry chef, had heard nothing of these stories, and when she started working at Mescalero in 1994, the last thing she was thinking of were ghosts. Rachel's job differed a bit from that of the usual kitchen staff. She worked early in the day, when the restaurant was not busy, and she typically worked alone, down in the basement. She had everything she needed there—a pastry bench, a pantry, the works—so she could spend entire days by herself unless someone intentionally came down to say hi.

It was a bit of a shock for Rachel the first time she had a paranormal encounter of her own. She was working hard in the basement as usual, trying to hit her targets for the day, when out of the corner of her eye she saw a woman with long, dark hair and wearing a blue dress, standing just past her left shoulder. Rachel spun around; no one was there, but she knew what she had seen. Unsure of what to do, she mentioned it to one of the serving staff, Kyle (who is still her best friend to this day). When she told Kyle about the mysterious visitor, he gave her a knowing look. "Of course," he told Rachel. "She was one of the brothel girls; she ended up getting shivved by one of her clients and died here."

After that first encounter, and realizing that the ghost was not interested in hurting her, Rachel was no longer afraid. It seemed that this attitude was all the encouragement this spectral young lady needed. She appeared often, several times a week, always in the periphery, never full on. Apart from that, she was a full-bodied

apparition, always dressed in the blue dress, and always with long, dark hair. This young woman wasn't just interested in popping up behind Rachel: she was seen kicking what looked like a stone around the basement; another time she was seen in the pantry, examining the shelves as if to see what was stored there. For Rachel she simply became part of the basement area, and she never felt scared or threatened by her.

Rachel moved on after working there almost a year. Not because of the ghost; she left simply because she had earned enough experience to further her career. But while Rachel moved on, she never forgot about the ghostly young woman she left behind.

MESCALERO/MAXINE'S IS NOW sadly a shell of what it once was—and I mean literally a shell; new condos were built inside the shell of the old building. What was once a piece of Vancouver history is now cladding for a condo building.

Will the stories stop now that the building has been gutted, or is the paranormal energy there attached to more than just a building? Perhaps it's tied to the site. This has been known to happen; an energy can be far more tethered to a location than to any structure. Sometimes the haunting can become more intense as the energy does not understand what is going on; at other times, people will simply experience odd emotions or strange feelings when in that shared space. Will the dark-haired young woman appear in the parking garage or in whatever retail establishment happens to open up in the bottom of the building? Will she go in peace now that the site of her death has been demolished, or will she stick around, tied to the last remnant that is now simply the heritage cladding on a modern building? Will she slowly vanish with nowhere to call her home?

POLTERGEIST IN A PIZZA PLACE

OST GHOST STORIES REQUIRE—OR SEEM TO, IN POPULAR lore—a musty, historical building, more than likely built by rich, old white people at least a hundred years ago. Not so with this one. The restaurant in this story is still in business, in a not-so-old mini mall. The owner, while comfortable enough when speaking about her experience, would rather not have it known that her restaurant is haunted; this is not your typical haunting.

"As a thirty-something," says Lisa, "I used to work in the most unassuming strip mall in North Vancouver. There's a pizza place close to the theatre, and I worked there as a store opener for just under a year. It was an excellent job, and it gave me a mental break from higher-stress work. I thoroughly enjoyed it, but it got weird pretty quickly.

"My shift started two hours before the store opened, and my duty was to make a day's worth of pizza, serve customers for one hour before the second staff member arrived, and then go to the back of the store to prep ingredients for the next day. I enjoyed the quiet time in the morning and was quite comfortable with the number of unusual occurrences around me. The store is up against a busy road as well as train tracks, so I never paid much mind to strange noises or bumps. It didn't take long to notice an energy or a presence around, and almost as soon as I did, things started happening.

"It began with the ingredient I didn't enjoy preparing: sliced garlic. To make a small batch, I would have to use a huge industrial slicer with many moving blades, and it was a nightmare to clean. The amount of garlic used on pizzas is relatively minimal, yet I always found myself having to prepare another batch. After the garlic was sliced and the blades were cleaned, I'd go to the fridge to put the garlic away and see the old batch exactly where it should be, clearly labelled.

"When I would make the pizzas, I did them in batches that used similar ingredients, putting anything I needed on the centre of the side table for easy access. Turning around one morning, I noticed the garlic tub had moved from the centre of the table to hanging off the side. My gut feeling was that whatever was hiding the garlic was now trying to dump it on the floor. The following morning, to test my theory, the only ingredient I put on the table was garlic, and from the corner of my eye, I saw it levitating about two inches, just hovering. More annoyed than scared, I demanded the garlic be put down because I wasn't going to make any more. That afternoon I talked with the store manager, who let me know she also believed the store to be haunted. After this conversation, the activity slowed for a little bit.

"On special mornings I'd have a school order, and instead of making 25 pizzas, I would have to make 225. It was always fun because I'd work with two other employees on a giant pizza assembly-line. On one of these special mornings, I was working with the manager and another young lady. The child-size pizzas were made, and we moved on to creating the regular day's worth of pizzas. We had not left each other's sides for the ninety minutes we had been in the store when I turned to the side table to look for the garlic, which had disappeared. The manager gave me a knowing look, and I left the group to see if I could find the missing ingredient. I checked all the fridges, the floor, and the back prep room; it was finally found in the customer lobby sitting in the centre of a table. For the garlic to be in the lobby, someone would've had to walk past us, walk through a noisy gate, and pass us a second time to put it down; this was quite impossible because we were alone. The young lady working with us understandably got quite upset, though we calmed her down enough that she agreed to go to the backroom to do the next day's prep, leaving the manager and me to talk.

"I told the manager that I believed the store had a poltergeist; it seemed plausible because most of the employees were in their teenage angst years. Lexi then opened up to me and began sharing her experiences managing this location. She had problems with the measuring cups disappearing in the middle of using them, as well as hearing footsteps and seeing boxes flying off racks; sometimes something would call her name while she was changing before her opening shift. As the manager, she also had to calm the staff after they experienced haunting activity, like having their personal belongings moved, seeing movement, or witnessing a hand or a small child out of the corner of their eye. Lexi had noticed that most of the activity happened when female staff were alone in the store. She said a past employee believed it was the spirit of a little boy that liked to play tricks, but it was nothing to worry about. The conversation wrapped up with us debating how a child spirit could end up at a pizza parlour in a strip mall. We concluded that with train tracks and industry right behind the store, and centuries of First Nations people living and working the land, a spirit could've come from anywhere.

"I still wasn't sure what was hiding the garlic, but I wanted to stop it. I reasoned that if it was a child, it could be bribed, and if it was a poltergeist, it couldn't, so I started to come to work with an assortment of small toys in my pocket. Each morning I would put a different toy on the side table to see if anything would happen. Nothing did until I brought an action figure (an articulated Teenage Mutant Ninja Turtles Raphael), and I found it on the floor over a foot and a half away from where it was sitting. If this toy attracted the entity's attention, it would move, show up somewhere else, or have its articulation slightly changed—and my garlic would stay put.

"Around this time, employees started to mention the ghost in the staff logbook, and the owner wasn't impressed. The owner didn't want us talking about it and probably believed if we stopped mentioning it, the hauntings would just go away.

"The next day, I came early to work and told whatever spirit was there to stop bothering the other staff. I invited it to hang out with me while I was working, and said I'd continue to bring a toy for it to play with, but the rule was it had to ignore the other staff; also, it wasn't allowed to follow me home, and it had to stop hiding the garlic. If it could follow these rules, I'd be its friend and keep it company. To my great astonishment, the spirit seemed to follow the rules.

"From that day on, I always felt a presence next to me at work, and it went away the second I left the building. To my surprise, the energy of the spirit wasn't draining, melancholy, or frightening in any way, making it comfortable for me to hold up my side of the deal. As I made pizzas in the morning, I would chat with the spirit like it was another employee, talking about the next task and thanking it for working so hard. By the time I was doing prep in the back, there was another employee in the store. I asked the spirit to sit on the corner of the table and quietly watch, explaining that we had to be silent around others. Weeks passed in comfort, sharing my time with an incredible spirit co-worker, and any time I opened the fridge or looked for an ingredient, it was always right at the front.

"My role as a pizza artist was never going to be a forever job, and I was upfront with the management that I was actively looking for work. When a job offer rolled in, the first 'person' I told was the spirit; I talked to them for a long time about it. I re-established the rules: the spirit wasn't allowed to follow me home, and I would still be its friend while I was working here. The energy felt physically closer to me those last days, and it seemed more intense when I was training the teenage girl replacing me.

"On my second-to-last day, I was in the back room with the trainee. The energy in the room at the time was so electric I was dumbfounded as I watched the young lady work, completely oblivious. My eyes kept going to the corner of the table, expecting to finally see the ghost for the first time because its power was on full blast. Instead, I perceived a question that the energy seemed to convey: *Is she going to talk to me?* My heart broke. I never thought about what the spirit was feeling.

"Owing my friend this much, I casually asked the girl, 'Hey do you believe in ghosts?' She responded no, with the passion of a skeptic who grew up in a house full of skeptics. I replied that it was probably good that she didn't believe in ghosts, and that many of the staff, including myself, felt the place was haunted. She replied again that there was no such thing, and then I realized that we were talking to an empty room—the energy left the room when I said it was good the trainee didn't believe in ghosts.

"On my last opening, I wasn't greeted by anyone, and I worked alone. It didn't stop me thanking the spirit for being such a good co-worker and friend, and I told it I hoped it could find a way home to its family. I never felt this spirit ever again.

"About a month later, I showed up at the restaurant one night to bring dinner home for my family. I was chatting with one of my old co-workers and asked how my replacement was doing. Turned out that she quit shortly after starting. She opened one morning, went into the back room, and saw a little boy sitting on the corner of the prep table. She turned around, left the restaurant, and never came back. My co-worker laughed and said, 'We've all had to deal with the ghost at one time, and we didn't quit because of it.' I commented that I felt sorry for her because she didn't believe in ghosts, and seeing a full apparition must have been terrifying. What I didn't tell any of my co-workers was that the exact spot she saw the apparition was where I'd tell my friend to hop up, be quiet, and watch me work."

VISITING THIS LOCATION myself was interesting. I definitely got a sense of something there, but nothing scary or mournful—it was more an impression of a young kid who wandered in and decided to stick around. Where did this energy come from? A casualty of the nearby railyards years ago? Someone who played too close to the river and was swept away? Maybe it was someone who died of the many sicknesses that were rampant in the early days of Vancouver's history, before modern medicine. In any case, I am grateful to have heard the story and to be able to share it with you.

IRVING HOUSE

T HE CITY OF NEW WESTMINSTER, NOW PART OF THE GREATER
Vancouver Area, was originally supposed to be *the* city, if
those who had a say in the matter had their way. The rivalry
between Victoria and New Westminster, as they vied for the position
of provincial capital, was heated and had supporters on both sides.
Unfortunately for New Westminster, Governor Douglas loved
Victoria and made it his home, and so, following some governmental
hijinks, Victoria became the capital of British Columbia in 1866,
even though New Westminster was the very first incorporated city in
the province. New Westminster further lost out when the terminus of
the railroad was set in the new city of Vancouver.

Captain William Irving was known as "King of the River"
because of his time on the Fraser River as a riverboat captain.
His home at 302 Royal Avenue in New Westminster is the oldest
standing house in the lower mainland. Built in 1865, the house is
open to the public, and visitors can view its original wallpaper, the
bed that Captain Irving died in, and lots of other pieces that are
original to the house and era. In April 1865, the house was described
by *British Columbian* newspaper as "the handsomest, the best and
most home-like house of which British Columbia can yet boast." Not
that anyone was gushing. In a city of hastily constructed houses, this
structure stood apart. The wood was brought in from California, and
no expense spared as it was to be the retirement home and display of
success for the good captain.

However, history is filled with stories of prestigious men who
built trophy homes only to have a short time during which to enjoy

them. Captain Irving and his wife Elizabeth joined the ranks of these hapless individuals: they only had a few years in the house before Captain Irving died at age fifty-six. During their marriage they had five children—four girls, and a boy who also became a riverboat captain after his father's death. Irving's widow Elizabeth went back to Oregon where she was from, but the house remained . . . and apparently Captain Irving remained with it.

There are a number of stories about Captain Irving lingering in his home. On some mornings it appears as if his bed has been slept in, although the house has been empty. One story involves a staff member who felt the long-dead captain brush past her on the stairs, muttering about making haste; that day happened to coincide with the date of his birth. Orbs and shadow people are quite regular in the house, and while the house is locked up tight, sometimes the security alarm will sense someone who simply isn't there and send out a warning, prompting all kinds of action by the living.

Other people have heard someone walking around upstairs when they're the only ones in the house, and it's quite normal for both visitors and staff to hear the sounds of someone going up or down the stairs or the door slamming shut. Even if you're looking straight at the unmoving door, it somehow makes the distinct sound of being opened and pulled shut behind someone as they leave. Some people are very uncomfortable in the house; the presence there is so strong. The staff have had groups of tourists walk in, with some of them immediately turning around and leaving. Sometimes they'll say, "No, I can't be in there," or "I'll wait for you guys outside." If pressed, they say it's because the presence in the house is very powerful and very clear about the ownership of the house. If you are sensitive to such things but are not comfortable with it, I would recommend either not going to the house or preparing yourself before you go, as you will feel this presence right away.

My friend Tani and I went to the house knowing nothing about

it. The house was closed, and there was no one there, so we walked around the outside. We wanted to get our own impressions of the site without prior knowledge or anyone telling us historical details that could skew our own impressions. We were rewarded for our efforts: I felt the presence of a man, specifically a man with a beard. He was kind but possessive and was obviously the owner of the house. He didn't mind us being there—he was used to welcoming many visitors to his home, but there was no doubt about whose house it was. As for Tani, she headed toward the back of the house, and in her mind heard the laughter of little girls, lots of them. She described a sense of joy and happiness and could feel the girls having a good time, feeling safe and loved. At the time this didn't make any sense, but once we read the history of the place we learned that the captain had five children, four of whom were girls. Is it the captain's energy that conjures up the girls, as if to recall them when he was there? I'm not sure, but I can tell you I could almost see them in my mind's eye playing on the property and having a great time.

Irving House is a gorgeous example of West Coast homes of the 1860s. If you haven't yet been to visit, I highly encourage you to do so. Just be prepared because in addition to the staff, you may sense the original resident wandering about in his handsome, well-loved home.

HAUNTED HOSPITALS

N MY YEARS OF COLLECTING GHOST STORIES, I HAVE NEVER heard of a hospital that is *not* haunted. Ever. Hospitals are places of strong spiritual energy because they are places of arrival and departures, much like an airport but with much longer-lasting consequences. I have many friends who work in the security industry, and they tell me there are places in *all* hospitals that they either prefer not to go to alone or that they avoid altogether.

Why are they so notably haunted? For much of the energy or spirits left behind it's going to be for the usual reasons. Sudden death and all its variations. For example: all they know is they collapsed at home and went unconscious having no idea that they are even in a hospital, let alone have died. Perhaps they came in for a simple operation, believing they'd be returning home the same day, but something went wrong, and they just never woke up. Maybe they are driving to work or home from a day out and a drunk driver they never see coming crashes in to them, and they're taken to the hospital where they later pass away.

So there you are, you have no idea where you are, you know something is very, very wrong, but you have no idea how to fix it. For many of them they're desperate to find their bodies, because that is at least one thing they know, but of course, it's too late. So where do they go now? If you don't realize you're dead, do you "move on" to the next plane of existence? Apparently, not everyone does, and that's why, in a place of healing and also death, there seems to be so many people left behind.

BURNABY HOSPITAL

WHILE THERE ARE COUNTLESS STORIES OF ENCOUNTERS with people who disappear into rooms, call buttons that ring the nurses' desk from seemingly empty rooms, and more, there's one story I was told by someone who had first-hand experience. It's such a compelling story that it was recreated for the television show *Haunted Hospitals*—and it is one of the most upsetting stories I've ever heard.

Glen Ferguson had recently arrived in Canada after serving with the British military for many years. He had seen action and things that people really shouldn't. He'd seen people at their best but more often their worst, as people often are in war zones and times of conflict. Glen was not someone who scared or even startled easily, so it seemed odd that it took an encounter as a security guard at Burnaby Hospital to not only shock him but to flat out terrify him.

Glen has been on many television shows and movies as a background actor, so he had a few stories to share about places that are no longer open to the general public. He also works as an investigator with Cornerstone Paranormal in Vancouver. This story was one of the first paranormal encounters he ever had, and I would think the most horrifying.

One night, the security guards at the hospital were asked to transfer the body of a recently deceased man to the refrigeration unit in the morgue. The deceased man was a German dancer who'd had a heart attack and was still in his traditional German clothes. The security guards didn't like dealing with the dead bodies; they preferred the ambulance crew do their own transfers. But the deceased

was a big guy, and the security guards decided it was easier if they did it themselves. They put a toe tag on the deceased and got him into a body bag. That's when Glen felt something right behind him touch his shoulder. He looked around and asked the other guard what he wanted, assuming it was him. The other guard looked at him strangely from across the room and said, "I haven't moved from this spot."

They got the gentleman into the cooler, locked up the morgue, and went about their regular patrols. That's when the odd activities began.

The motion alarm went off in the morgue, which was strange because it was the first time in three years that anything had happened to trigger the alarm. According to the security guard monitoring the different security screens, there was an open cooler door in the morgue that they had just left. The monitoring guard radioed Glen and told him to go close the door and secure the area. So he headed down to investigate the fridge while his partner turned off the alarm. Glen suspected someone might have broken in the back door to mess with the bodies, but there was no one there.

They secured the area, called it in as a false alarm, and headed back to their patrols. Then the alarm went off again. This time, Glen went down to investigate on his own, feeling annoyed that he had to bother with it again.

When he reached the morgue, he walked into the cooler room, and when he was well inside the room, the door slammed shut as if someone had pushed it closed from the inside. It's worth noting that the door did not close automatically; it had to be manually closed. And then the lights went out. Like the door, the lights had to be manually turned off—this was before motion sensor lights.

Glen was understandably unsettled, but then things got even worse. Standing in the cooler room in the dark, with the door shut behind him, he started to freak out. Then there was rustling from one of the body bags. Then more rustling and crackling. Glen pressed his back against one of the walls, then slid down to the floor. "Something was going on in that morgue that I couldn't describe," he told me.

At this point, Glen's eyes had adjusted enough that he could see the body bag moving—the bag that Glen and his partner had just zipped up over the body of the deceased German dancer. It was as if the man was trying to get out of the bag.

That was when he fully began to panic. Glen just wanted to get out, but he couldn't see enough to find his way, and in the dark he'd become disoriented. He flicked on his lighter to try to cast some sort of light, and that's when he heard the zipper sliding down on the body bag. Glen was now completely panicked and started groping around in the dark to find his way out.

He had feared his own death in combat and had seen enough death for a lifetime, but this was by far the most terrifying situation he had ever been in. Just as Glen reached the door, things took a turn for the worse. When he turned around, he could see a man standing in the corner with a hood up. Glen described him to me as a dark figure, a shadow figure. He could still see the body bag moving next to him. Then it felt like the dark figure was moving toward him, and that was when Glen started screaming. It was the most scared he'd ever been in his life. Finally, after groping in the dark for what seemed like forever, Glen found the door handle, opened the door, and took off down the hall.

After calming himself, he informed his supervisor, who responded with disbelief and skepticism. Glen left that night a different man from the one who had gone to work earlier that day. Once he got home and finally went to bed, he had nightmares about the event, and continued to for weeks. In these nightmares, Glen was back in the morgue, and the hooded figure was there as well. It would reach over and unzip the bag, and the German man would sit up, turn and look at Glen, and scream, "Why?" It all became too much. Glen was unable to go down to the morgue after that night, and he ended up leaving the hospital and took a job in public transportation.

To this day, Glen knows that what he experienced was genuine. If people don't believe him, he says, well, they need to experience it first-hand before passing judgment.

So, what was it that Glen saw down in the cooler? What happened to make it such a terrifying experience? My thought is this: Many cultures believe that the dead don't leave their bodies right away; either they're waiting for the next step, or they simply don't know what else to do. This may explain the presence that Glen felt while zipping the deceased man into the body bag. Perhaps it was the deceased trying to get his attention. As he had died with no warning, it may have been that the deceased felt it was all a mistake and that he needed help to get out of that situation. Regardless, the hooded figure would be terrifying in any circumstance, and Glen felt nothing but relief to get out of there; he says, "I've never been in a morgue since that night, and I never will again." And really, can you blame him?

Glen is now an experienced paranormal investigator, and as time has passed, a pattern has emerged: If there is an entity about, it seems to go straight for him. I'm not sure why—after all, Glen is a straightforward, relatively relaxed man—but for some reason, he has been attacked by entities at other locations. I find it utterly terrifying that someone with such a laid-back personality could attract these energies.

VANCOUVER GENERAL HOSPITAL

V ANCOUVER GENERAL HOSPITAL MAY BE ONE OF THE MOST haunted hospitals on the West Coast; its long history probably has something to do with it.

Vancouver General started out as a tent in 1886, with a capacity for nine patients. It was created by the Canadian Pacific Railroad and was primarily for the treatment of railroad workers, who were busy building the railroad and getting blown up, crushed, buried in sudden rock slides, and generally sacrificing everything for the push of national unity—and, of course, for profit. The makeshift hospital was destroyed later that same year in the Great Vancouver Fire that ravaged the city on June 13. A new single-storey cottage hospital was built, and soon after, the City of Vancouver took it over and named it City Hospital. In 1888, a new building was erected with a thirty-five-patient capacity. It soon became a compound of brick buildings with wooden balconies and had wards for male and female patients. There were electric lights in the operating rooms and steam heat for sterilizing equipment, and the city morgue became part of the compound. In 1902, a board of directors was put in charge; that is when the compound was given the new and current name of Vancouver General Hospital. Like most hospitals in urban centres, Vancouver General Hospital has had many additions over the years, with new specialty buildings constructed for specific purposes and to treat specific ailments.

Kelly, a nurse of nearly twenty years, told me extraordinary tales about her time at the hospital. She is a no-nonsense kind of woman, but then again, I find most nurses have an unflappable, easygoing nature that overlays a steely, strong core; my mom was a nurse for many years, so I have a bit of inside knowledge when it comes to the profession. Kelly, a pragmatic individual, is not the kind of person you would expect to tell you ghostly tales.

Kelly has experienced phenomena while people are dying and after they have died (though such experiences are not limited to these moments). She says that people who are dying see things that could be dismissed as part of the brain losing its power, but oftentimes it truly appears to be departed loved ones helping the ailing patient cross over to the other side. The nature of these instances is so consistent that Kelly has become a believer. And the people who have died, she says, hang around for a bit. Sometimes a room in which someone has recently died—a room now empty and awaiting sterilization before a new patient is brought in—has a call button that is repeatedly activated for a few hours or even the entire night after the former patient has died. It's as if a very confused and insistent person is trying to call the nurse for help. Kelly says that after a while the noise seems to slow down and then stop, but sometimes it goes longer and sometimes shorter—she can never predict it. However, this is not the rule, but the exception. Kelly has seen countless people draw their last breath; most of them exit peacefully and without residual energy trying to get anyone's attention.

Kelly is circumspect about specifying locations in the hospital where different occurrences have taken place; she does not want to encourage people to scout around for paranormal experiences. However, she did share some stories of things she's experienced in her years working all over the hospital complex.

In one ward, she told me, there was often "the other nurse," as patients called her. This kindly spirit would often attend to Kelly's patients before she did. They would claim the other nurse had already been there and poured them water, fluffed their pillows, and on one occasion assisted someone to the bathroom. While this certainly lightened Kelly's load, it was a bit disconcerting to know she was working with someone who simply wasn't there in the living world. When asked to describe her, the patients were consistent in their descriptions: she was young, pretty, with dark hair, wearing an older style nurse uniform; in fact, when patients commented to the "other nurse" about her outfit, she would merely smile.

Does this young nurse know she's gone? What draws her back? My mother always said that nursing was a vocation, not a job, so perhaps this young woman feels the same. Maybe she feels that death is not going to break her vocation, so she'd better do a good job.

When Kelly transferred off the ward, the "other nurse" did not come with her, but seemed to remain attached to the ward, according to the other (living) nurses working there.

Another spirit Kelly would run into was not as pleasant; this spirit was on the elevator and seemed angry. Kelly would board the elevator to go to wherever she needed, and the doors would close and off they'd go. But somewhere along the way, a dark or angry-seeming energy would arrive in the elevator. The first time it happened, Kelly said she was looking over her shoulder and could see a shadow where she felt someone was standing. It never left the elevator first; it would always still be there when Kelly got to her floor and got off the elevator, but it was never waiting for her, either—it always showed up in transit. Kelly had the strong sense that this was a man, and while she never felt he was angry with her, she also never wasted any time once the elevator had got to her floor.

The last consistent spirit that Kelly still experiences is that of an older man. It doesn't seem that he's a patient, but rather that he's visiting someone who most likely is long gone now. Kelly and other nurses have seen him shuffle down the hall, quite late at night, with a long brown coat, black shoes, and a 1940s-style hat. He always has a newspaper tucked under his arm and never seems to be in that much of a hurry, yet when they make a move to go after him, he's gone.

When telling her stories, Kelly did not seem all that bothered by anything she had seen or heard while working in the hospital. Like many in her profession, she considers it just part of the job, but she did say there are some stories she really can't share with anyone but her husband because she is worried people would think she's mentally unstable. Thankfully she shared some of them with me— and now you, the reader—and it's a great reminder that if we think we know exactly what's going on in a location, there's always room for surprises.

Life is a series of arrivals and departures, including our own. Almost all of us begin and end our lives in hospitals, one way or the other. While some of these stories can be unsettling, it's comforting to realize that these places house the natural continuum of life and death, of which we all partake together.

RIVERVIEW HOSPITAL

MENTAL HOSPITALS, AT ONE TIME MORE COMMONLY referred to as insane asylums, never seem to get away with *not* being haunted—it seems to come with the territory. Perhaps the psychically scattered energy left behind has no idea that it's supposed to move. Maybe the deceased person is thrilled to finally have the freedom they so craved in life and can see no reason to move on. Sometimes, perhaps in cases of severe mental illness, the person may not even realize they have died. In any case, facilities across North America and Europe that have housed the mentally distressed always seem to end up with more than their fair share of spirits, kindly, curious, mischievous, or just downright terrifying.

Riverview Hospital, now closed, is currently a collection of unused buildings on a sprawling piece of property in Coquitlam. In 1904, the provincial government purchased over one thousand acres to build the facilities as the mental health care facility in Victoria was too full; between Victoria and Vancouver, there was a tremendous demand for mental health facilities, and the overcrowding of the facilities that did exist was shocking.

The Coquitlam property, in a rural area at the time, also housed a farm that had been purchased as part of the land deal. This farm was quickly put to use, and through patient labour it produced over seven hundred tons of crops and twenty thousand gallons of milk. A plant nursery, arboretum, and botanical garden were all added to the grounds, again through patient labour as it was thought to have therapeutic value. I might think the same thing if I was getting that much free work out of people.

Riverview expanded over the next few decades, adding on another building known as East Lawn, for those who were categorized as "acute female patients." Another building, called Centre Lawn, was added to house and treat those with the most serious mental health issues. Soon there was a building called North Lawn, for those with tuberculosis, and multiple residences for nurses, doctors, and other staff were constructed. Then there were buildings such as a sewage pumping station, a power station, and structures for the cemetery and grounds equipment.

At its peak, the hospital as a whole was the provider of care to a staggering 4,300 patients. Its decline began in the 1960s with the wider distribution of antipsychotic medications and an ongoing belief that people would do better in the community (if medicated) rather than locked up in a facility. The decline continued until 2004, when Riverview was reduced to eight hundred beds; many of those were now for the care of the elderly and less for the care of mental health patients.

A large parcel of Riverview's land was sold off to a developer, further shrinking the footprint of the once massive hospital, and the facility's function slowly ground to a halt. Smaller buildings were built for the ongoing care of the most intensive mental health patients, but the large, iconic buildings have all been shut down. That said, some of the buildings on the property are used to this day, but for an entirely different purpose.

In 2005, a good number of television and movie productions began using the former East Lawn building for filming. Supernatural shows as well as action movies couldn't get enough of the old building, which seemed to give off an aura of power and intimidation. As productions were being set up within its walls, reports that things were not quite right started to emerge.

Back when Riverview was active, there were tunnels that connected the buildings, used to move supplies back and forth—and to quietly remove the dead without upsetting other patients; the morgue was on the lower level, so the tunnels made even more sense. A few years ago, when an individual working onsite for a television show had to go through the tunnels, she grew increasingly unnerved because as she began her journey the water pipes began banging. *Okay*, she thought, *old buildings, old pipes, no problem.* But as she got deeper into the tunnel, the banging grew louder and more frequent. It sounded as if someone was trying to hammer their way out. At this point the employee thought, *Forget this*, and she turned around and headed back the way she had come. As she did this, the banging ceased. This freaked her out far more than if the banging had continued.

The energy in the tunnels had more than one reaction to those who passed through them. Sam was the night guard for one particular movie set, and he was required to patrol throughout East Lawn and ensure that no one would get into the set or steal anything. One of the places he had to go to was the tunnels.

"I hated those tunnels," he says. "Every time I was in there I would hear whispers, giggles, even laughing, but the worst was the footsteps. I would know I was there alone, and I knew no one else was on the property, but I would be down in those tunnels and hear someone walking about five or six feet behind me, in hard-soled shoes. Whenever I had to go down there I would almost run—I hated those tunnels so bad, and it never got any better."

(I find it interesting that Sam would end his account with "it never got any better," because I've observed that in some cases the energy seems to get used to you, tolerate you, or even feel positive toward you, enough that it would rather play jokes on you than scare you. But that was not the case for Sam.)

Will, one of the employees who'd worked on multiple television shows, was onsite at the Riverview buildings for long stretches of time, sometimes for many months. He says his time in East Lawn wasn't quite as terrifying as it had been for others, but he suspects his attitude toward it all was able to turn the unsettling activity around a bit.

He told me the usual stories about hearing noises in empty rooms, as well as shuffling, footsteps, disembodied voices—all the things other people had experienced. As a set decorator, he needed to be in different parts of the building at times when other people often weren't, so he got quite used to being there alone. Sometimes Will would have to use the elevator to move pieces of scenery or carts of set dressing from one floor to another, but oftentimes something else had other plans for Will's elevator journey. He would load up the elevator, and instead of going to the second or third floor as intended he would find himself in the basement, where the elevator doors would open—and remain open. The first time it happened, he figured that since the elevator was old it must be malfunctioning, but that wasn't the case. Will could hit all the buttons he wanted, but nothing would cause the elevator to move or the doors to close.

On one such occasion, he grew increasingly frustrated and thought he was going to have to unload the elevator in the basement and haul the set pieces up the stairs by hand; understandably, the prospect left him grumpy. After pushing buttons with no results, he loudly huffed, "Oh, just go already, give me a break!" With that, the doors closed, and the elevator headed to the third floor where Will had wanted to go in the first place. This was not an isolated incident, and if it was nighttime and Will was on his own, the chances of such disruptions were much higher. Will soon learned that all he needed to do on one of the hijacked elevator trips was to say something like, "Okay, very funny, can we go up now?" The doors would then close as if voice-activated, and the elevator would go on its way.

"I didn't feel particularly scared of it, to be honest," he says. "I simply accepted it was there and worked with it." It's that kind of attitude that has allowed Will to work on multiple productions filmed in the old East Lawn building when many others have simply refused to come back, or in some cases quit in the middle of the job.

Kelly, a night security guard with years of experience under her belt, had a completely different experience. She was not someone who believed in the paranormal; rather, she always believed there was a logical explanation for everything. As far as she was concerned everything fit in a nice neat box . . . until Riverview. While she has had some odd experiences in her time, she has never experienced any place as blatantly and actively haunted as this one.

Kelly was, at first, thrilled to get the Riverview gig; it was a solid eight-hour shift with no responsibilities other than to patrol the abandoned hospital site, making it a quiet environment with no members of the public to deal with. When she was on shift, there were no filming projects going on, so the site was silent and empty. Kelly had done one evening shift there already, but the second night was very different. (In retrospect, she tells me, she realizes that during that quiet first shift, the spectral energies were sizing her up.)

On her second shift, just as Kelly began her patrol through the building, she saw the shadow of someone ahead of her duck into a room. This put her on alert, naturally. "You'll have to come out of there," she called out, "and I'll need to escort you from the building." She got a quick glimpse of the person, if only from behind: a tall, thin, slightly balding man, wearing what looked like pyjamas.

She approached the room she'd seen the mystery man go into, tightening her grip on her flashlight in case she needed it to double as a weapon. Kelly stepped into the room, ready to deal with whatever she found, but discovered nothing. There wasn't even a piece of furniture in there—no closet, no bathroom, nothing at all. Kelly left the room feeling confused; she had, without a doubt, seen a man go in there.

As Kelly made her way through the building, working her way down different levels, she kept hearing voices, laughter, and footsteps, loud and clear enough that she would turn around. Kelly had an unnerving sense of being watched; it was as if she had walked into a crowd of people she couldn't see but knew were there. When coming down the stairs from the second to the first floor Kelly stumbled, not because her boot caught on anything, but because she had the distinct feeling of two hands on her back giving her a good, hard shove. She caught herself from tumbling down the stairs, but at this point her nerve was quickly deserting her. By the time Kelly got to the ground floor and was now supposed to go to the basement, she knew that was just not going to happen.

Not only did Kelly leave the building, but she also left the property. She sat in her car, parked near the gate, until her shift was over. Then she drove to the headquarters of the security firm and told them that she would not be returning to Riverview and that she needed a new assignment. There was no way this non-believer was ever going back there.

GLEN FERGUSON, THE local ghost investigator referred to elsewhere in this book, works as a background actor on many of the shows and movies shot at the hospital. He would often go on impromptu ghost hunts in between takes. After one such adventure, he came back to the dressing room to get changed. A fellow actor who was with him looked at Glen's leg and said something along the lines of, "Your wife got pretty wild last night, eh?"

When Glen looked down, he saw a clearly defined bite mark that had not been there before his ghost hunt less than hour before. Glen showed me the picture—there is no mistaking what it is: a perfectly visible bite mark made by a full set of top and bottom teeth. Frankly, I would have called it a day right there and headed home, but Glen is braver than I am. He had felt nothing, as is often the case with suspected ghostly assaults; in such instances, scratches or bruises will sometimes appear on people who don't recall feeling anything or injuring themselves in any way.

Different people experience different sides of any haunting. Our own attitudes and possibly our own fear level seem to fuel or calm whatever entity may be residing in a place; this would explain the difference in experiences had by Will and Kelly. Perhaps the spirits got used to Will and saw him as someone to play with, while Kelly was seen as an intruder.

There are many stories about the experiences people have had in East Lawn and Riverview. East Lawn is not open to the public, and there are fences around some of the older buildings, but when I got as close as I could to the place, I had a strong sense of sadness, abandonment, and confusion. The people who lived out their lives there were taken care of, or at least supervised their entire lives, and suddenly found themselves alone in the spirit world. It's no wonder they're not the most welcoming of entities when in their minds they have been left to rot along with the place they called home.

The future of East Lawn is uncertain; I suppose it will be used for filming movies and television shows for as long as it can be. The Riverview complex, smaller now, continues to be used for health-care and the treatment of addictions. I can't help but wonder what will come next for this incredibly haunted and substantial piece of Greater Vancouver's history.

THE GROUSE GRIND

WHAT STARTED OUT AS A CHALLENGING FOOTPATH HAS turned into one of the most popular places for fit, active people looking for a challenge that can be tackled in ninety minutes or so for the average hiker.

At 2.9 kilometres, it's not that the Grouse Grind is long—it's more that it's a relentless journey *up*. Nicknamed "Nature's Stairmaster," the trail has been in use since 1982, but Grouse Mountain itself is no stranger to human activity either.

The first hikers arrived at the top of the mountain in 1892 and named it after the birds that seemed to be the most popular in the area. The first lodge was built by Scandinavians, avid hikers in the 1920s. In the 1930s a toll road went in, and soon there was a village made up of a group of cabins at the base of the mountain, and a ski run, also situated near the base. The first chair lift was installed in 1949, and this kicked off growth for the top part of the mountain, with the current facilities showing up in the 1990s.

As for the Grouse Grind, it got a more formalized look in the early 1980s when Don McPherson and Phil Severy cleared a single-person footpath up the mountain. It made for a challenging trail, but hikers could save their knees by taking the gondola back down the mountain rather than descending on foot. The trail grew more and more popular and was formalized in the 1990s, better marked, and wide enough that people could safely pass each other going up or down in a safe and orderly way. Today, the average number of people per year doing the Grouse Grind is more than 100,000.

But not everyone who has started the trail has completed it.

There have been at least eleven deaths on the trail since 1999. For some, death came for those who were not fit enough to make the trip, bringing on heart attacks; others have died from misadventure—anything from slipping and falling, to getting lost and dying of exposure or hypothermia, or getting caught up in a natural event like an avalanche. In any case, a good many deaths on the Grind have happened suddenly, and for this reason, the experiences of the living people who hike the Grind sometimes seem to bump up against the stories of those who never made it home.

When people die suddenly—by accident, a crime, a medical event, things of this nature—it seems that their chances of becoming a ghost increase. If someone is not aware that they are deceased they may try to finish what they started, or at the very least try to get home only to find themselves stuck. Does this explain the odd situations people have experienced while doing the Grind themselves?

More than one person has reported the feeling of someone following them up the trail, but even with repeated checking they find that they are entirely alone. They often write this off as perhaps an animal watching them, or they speculate that maybe they're just faster than whoever may be back there; when they reach the top, no one even remotely close emerges from the trail. Similarly, people report being sure they hear someone ahead of them, the foot falls making a distinctive sound as they hit the stairs built into the mountain, but they can't see anyone there. It seems that whether you are going up or down, and whether you're ahead or behind, the trail is never truly empty.

Two residents of the Grouse Mountain area shared their experience with me. Living in such close proximity to the mountain, the two women would often hike the trail together in the summer. On one such trip, they looked up the mountain and clearly saw a man a few metres ahead who had not been there when they started out. He hiked a short way and then seemed to blink out of existence, like a light bulb turning off. Both women described him the same way: older, with short greying hair, wearing a white shirt, black shorts, and running shoes.

Sean, a young man who lives in Vancouver, has hiked the Grind only a few times, but he had a bit more of a disconcerting experience. He was coming down the mountain just as it was getting close to dark. He was a student at the time and was unwilling to pay the ticket price to get back down the mountain on the gondola, so he would hike up, grab some water at the washrooms up top, and then hike back down. On this particular hike, he'd spent a little too much time at the top of the mountain; it was an exceptionally clear day, and he could see farther than usual. As a result, he lingered longer than he should have. Realizing the time, he was concerned about getting back down the mountain in daylight hours, so he was in a bit of a rush as he headed down the trail he'd emerged from that same day.

Sean says he was about a quarter of the way down the now-abandoned trail when he heard a man's voice call, "Help!"

Sean stopped, unsure of what he'd heard, and listened harder.

Again he heard the voice call, "Help!"

Sean called back, "Where are you? What do you need?"

There was no response.

"Hello?" Sean called again. Still nothing. He figured he must have misheard, and began to go down the trail again—and that's when he heard it again. He left the trail to go toward the voice, hoping he could find it. "Hello," he called. "What's wrong? Where are you?"

Again, no response.

Just as Sean had reached the spot where he thought he'd heard the call from, it came again, but this time, just as far away into the bush as it had been the first time. The voice sounded exactly the same, and exactly the same distance away as when Sean had been on the path. It was at that point that Sean felt like he was being lured off the path, and with the light waning he assumed it couldn't be for a good reason. He couldn't explain why he felt that way, other than it felt very, very wrong and that he was in danger. So Sean headed back to the path and decided he would report the incident when he got to the base of the trail.

He made it off the mountain and got back to his car, where he'd left his phone (he'd wanted to unplug and carry as little as possible on his climb) and he called in his experience. There had been no reports of anyone missing yet, and so far that week anyone who'd gone up the mountain had come back down, but they had Sean describe where he'd been in case a search was required.

Sean has hiked the Grouse Grind many times since but has never had that sort of thing happen again.

In 2013, *Outside* magazine listed the Grouse Grind as one of the world's top ten most dangerous hikes. Many people are surprised to hear this, but that may be because as West Coast residents we grow complacent about the power of nature and forget that it is to be respected, taken seriously, and even feared when appropriate. We tame pieces of the mountains for our entertainment or exercise, forgetting the real danger that we could be in when we set off up the side of a mountain to reach the top. The Grouse Grind proves that even a monitored, maintained, popular, and heavily travelled trail can still exact a price.

I encourage you to remember those who were lost on this trail as you hike up the mountain. Always show respect for the side of nature we think we have declawed. Unlike a river or lake, the dangers of a mountain might not be immediately apparent, but it doesn't make them or the people they have claimed any less real.

A PRIVATE HOME NEAR GROUSE MOUNTAIN

G ROUSE MOUNTAIN IS NOT ONLY A POPULAR RECREATIONAL spot for Vancouverites year round—there are many lovely homes nearby in Vancouver's North Shore region.

I usually try to give an approximate location or at least a block number when I share a story of a haunted location, but the family who agreed to share this story did not want people driving by their home out of morbid curiosity. The entire family agrees that their house is haunted; each has had experiences individually as well as together as a whole. One member of the family decided not to share her experiences because when she started to write them down for me, the activity in the house suddenly picked up, and that was the last thing she wanted.

The house was built in the 1950s and was owned by a husband and wife who appear to have lived there the rest of their lives until the current owners bought it in the late seventies. It also seems that the original couple have decided they're not going anywhere, even with the current (living) owners in the home. The wife seems sweet, taking a polite interest in what's going on around her and making the odd noise or movement from time to time. The husband, however, has a different temperament; the energy he gives off is arrogant, nosy, and controlling.

The current owners' daughter-in-law, Lily, shares how she came across the ghost; her husband, Vimes, also has stories to tell about his experiences in his childhood home:

"In 2000 I met a wonderful man," says Lily, "and he brought me to his childhood home to meet his family. They were lovely, but the family home seemed a little off. It featured seventies' architecture, with large rooms and lots of exposed wood; it was filled with antiques and a view of the entire North Shore and Vancouver and, on a clear day, Vancouver Island. Indeed it was, and is, a stunning home. The house's main feature is a wall of windows to highlight the vast views, yet the house can feel dark, almost like there isn't enough light.

"As our relationship blossomed, I was treated to many delicious meals in this home, but the house started feeling darker the more I visited. I learned there were areas I preferred to be and places that I didn't feel comfortable. The entire downstairs and upstairs hallway were spots that I sped through, yet the formal living room felt warm and friendly. Avoiding the awkward question of whether this place was haunted, I asked about the living room, saying how nice it was; that is when I learned it was added after the original construction. All of my favourite rooms were from additions made by my future in-laws.

"I chalked up any odd feelings I had to being nervous and wanting to make a good impression, but my perception changed after the first Christmas. It was a perfect European holiday, right down to lighting candles on the Christmas tree and singing songs together around the piano. We were not yet married, so I went downstairs to sleep in the guest room, and my partner went to sleep in his childhood room. He had a restful night while I met the house ghost.

"Once I was tucked into bed, I instinctively knew I wasn't alone. Seeing ghosts is rare for me, but I can often feel energy and know the intention of spirits. Whatever was in the room with me was curious and wasn't emitting friendly, happy vibes. My hope was that it would stay in the corner of the room and not come closer. Typically, in such a scenario, I would psychically surround myself in protection, but I had been drinking and wasn't capable of doing much. I was aware the spirit was a man, and he was now standing right next to the bed and was leaning over me as if to give a kiss. This didn't feel loving, but rather possessive, and I knew I was sleeping in his house.

"Weighing my options, I decided that I could handle a ghost better than an upset future mother-in-law, so I wasn't going to sneak upstairs for safety. I told whatever was in the room with me that I knew he was there, and that he wasn't permitted to touch me. I pulled the sheets over my eyes and went to sleep. Generally, if I ignore a spirit, they get bored and move on, but I woke twice in the night to pee, and he hadn't moved. I held it till I heard someone up at 7:00 AM, so I used the bathroom and went to join my future mom in the kitchen for a much-needed cup of coffee.

"I told my partner about the incident on the way to my home, insisting that I would never sleep alone in the house again. Luckily I didn't have to. My partner let me know that there were two ghosts in the house, and his family believed they were the original couple who built it. Knowing that others had experiences let me work past it, and I became more comfortable in the home.

"Years later, we were sitting around the dining table with my sister-in-law (my husband's sister) and her new husband. I asked the newest family member if he enjoyed his sleep in the basement bedroom. He shrugged and said it was fine, and I joked that at least he didn't see the ghost watching him. He laughed, but my sister commented that yes, he had been watched the times he had slept over. She described the same experiences that I had had on my first Christmas in the house. It appeared that whatever was in the house was curious about new people. We had an open conversation with the whole family about the experiences in the home; even Dad, who doesn't believe in the paranormal, admitted to hearing footsteps in the upstairs hall. The following day, Mom went downstairs and had a stern conversation with the spirit, telling him to leave her family alone.

"Over the last twenty years the house energy has ebbed and flowed, but it is never as bad as it was the first Christmas. Recently we asked Mom if we could share some of the house stories; she agreed, but she refrained from sharing her own. The activity has picked up in the last year to the point where a spirit actually touched her, and she doesn't want to encourage more of that."

Vimes says, "When I was about nine or ten, I had the same nightmare for several days in a row. It involved a menacing black form chasing me. The form was a human shape made out of a blackness so dark it felt like it was sucking in all light. It had no face, just a black hole where one should be. I would run and run, but no matter what I did, the pursuer was relentless. This would wake me up crying, and often my body was 'running' under my blankets.

"The first time this happened, I tried to fall back asleep, but as soon as I closed my eyes, I would immediately see its 'face,' so I would try to stay awake. The second time it happened, I cried so loudly that my mom came to check on me. I told her about my nightmare, but she assured me that it was only a dream and told me to try to think of happy things to help me fall asleep. I tried this, but no matter what I did, the figure would always find me, and I would end up running into my parents' bedroom for safety.

"After several nights of this happening, my mom and I began to pray a simple prayer of protection every night before bed. This helped, but eventually the figure entered my dreams, and again I woke up. When this happened, I would repeat the prayer to myself until I fell asleep. Eventually I started dreaming about praying whenever the monster came for me, and it finally gave up. My mom and I continued this ritual for many years after, and luckily it never occurred again. I still get unnerved when I think about it.

"A few years later, when I was twelve years old, my favourite toy was a Lieutenant Falcon G.I. Joe action figure. I played with it every day. The few times it wasn't being played with, it was proudly displayed on my bookshelf so I could see it from anywhere in my room.

"One night my parents had a party, so I spent the evening at a friend's house. When I got home, the first thing I noticed was that the action figure was gone. Nothing else in my room was disturbed, yet Lieutenant Falcon was nowhere to be found. I looked all over the house, but it had vanished.

"I approached my mom and told her what happened and accused someone at her party of having stolen it. She was incredulous and asked me why an adult would steal a G.I. Joe. I had to agree with her—but where, then, had it gone?

"Over the ensuing days, I continued to look for the figure but never found it. Years later, Lieutenant Falcon was still missing when I boxed up all my childhood toys. Eventually, when I moved out of my parents' house, I hoped it might appear, but it never did."

Vimes went on to tell me stories about the bells in the home:

"Our living room and kitchen are attached. There is a set of three hanging cowbells mounted on a wall by the dinner table; my mother would ring them to tell us that food was ready. The three bells surround a central handle that you used to chime out *do-re-me*; unless they are struck with the handle, these bells remain silent.

"Somewhere between 1989 and 1990, my parents, sister, and I were all watching *Unsolved Mysteries* in the living room. It was a particularly spooky segment, and we muted the commercial so we could talk about it. Our talking stopped when one single bell rang out clearly. This wasn't my mother calling us for dinner—the whole family was together, and we were all staring at the bells.

"Curious, we went to inspect them. The handle wasn't swinging, and there were no open windows on this crisp autumn night. Nothing we could see could explain how it had rung. We started coming up with rational theories, but each became more unlikely. Then my sister suggested, "Maybe it was a large moth that rang the bell!" She bumped the handle like a moth would have, but the bells remained silent.

"Immediately I thought that it was something supernatural but didn't want to voice my opinion. I'm confident we all felt the same way (I know my sister did), but we just kind of went with the attitude of *well, that happened,* and then we went back to watching our TV show."

And then, Vimes says, there was the Ghost Lady:

"In the early 1990s my sister moved out, and her room was turned into the computer room. The computer desk was facing the door, which looked into the hallway. The hallway runs from the kitchen to the bedrooms.

"One evening, before dinner, I was entranced by a game of *Civilization.* Out of the corner of my eye I saw a misty, smoke-like, grey, human shape float past the doorway, then down the hallway toward my parents' room. It went so slowly and deliberately that I fully saw a short 'grey lady.'

"I was dumfounded and called out, 'Mom?' but there was no answer. If it was Mom, I would have heard her bedroom door open, but I'd heard nothing. Carefully—because I was frightened—I got up to look down the hallway, but nothing was there. So I booked it to the kitchen, where I found my mom cooking dinner. I asked her if she had just gone to her room. Obviously she hadn't as she was in the middle of creating a meal. After telling her what I had seen, we both agreed it was very strange. Thankfully, that was my only ghost sighting in the house."

Vimes concluded his series of stories with a tale about mysterious recurring footsteps:

"When you're in the basement, you can sometimes hear the sound of footsteps, which seem to go down the hallway. My dad described it as someone walking with a limp or with a cane; my mom described heavy footsteps.

"Once, when Mom was at home alone, the steps were so clear it caused her to run to the neighbour's house. The neighbour looked everywhere for an intruder but found no one. I've heard them once or twice; it's as if the original homeowner is walking with a cane down the hallway he built."

GROWING UP IN a haunted house could not have been easy for Vimes, but he seems to have taken it in stride, accepting it as a part of his childhood home. External appearances would have you believe that this house was just like all the other ones on the street, in a regular neighbourhood that could be anywhere, but no—*this* house was haunted. It goes to show that you never know what's really going on in a home. I'd say there's probably at least one haunted house in your neighbourhood, too.

WATERFRONT STATION

I T SEEMS APPROPRIATE THAT THE BUILDING CREATED TO BE the literal end of the line for the Canadian Pacific Railroad is anything but the end for a few spectral passengers who will never reach their ultimate destination.

The current building, built in 1914, retains its original name and role as transportation hub, but everything else about it has changed over the last century and beyond. It ran as a train station until 1979; in 1978 it shifted from CPR to Via Rail, which used the beautiful structure for just a year before consolidating operations elsewhere.

Over the years, Waterfront Station has evolved to meet the needs of the growing city and region. Used extensively during Expo '86 and during the 2010 Olympics, the station has had a long history of moving vast numbers of people—not just around the country, but all over the region, as seen more recently.

What is it about train stations, subway stations, and bus stations that attracts so much spiritual attention? Many older public trans-portation buildings are haunted; I believe it's because there's a non-stop river of people spending time and energy in these places, pondering things like, *Am I doing the right thing? Will they still feel the same way about me when I get there? What if it doesn't work out? I haven't seen them in so long, I can't wait to get there. If I'm not successful at this meeting, I don't have any other options.*

There are more than a few places here at Waterfront where you can come face to face with the paranormal. An unknown woman has been reported entering the women's washroom, but never coming out. Other travellers describe hearing someone come in when the

washroom is only occupied by themselves, but finding when they leave their stall that no one else is in there with them. However, they know what they heard: it was a woman's footsteps, in high heels, clicking her way into the bathroom; a stall is then shut and locked, then silence. So why is it that when the living traveller emerges from their own stall, all the other stall doors remain ajar, and the person is totally alone?

The stairs closest to this washroom have had security guards scratching their heads for years. One security guard I spoke to told me surveillance cameras often show people going up and down those stairs, even when the station is known to be empty. This is bad news for the security staff as it means they have to go to the stairwell to check it out. But to this day they have never seen a living person on the stairs in the middle of the night—there's simply no one there. What's more, the station is plagued by motion sensor alarms that seem to trip themselves all on their own, but when the dutiful security guard arrives at the location of the tripped alarm, there is inevitably no one there.

Trains and train stations in general can be dangerous, and despite all precautions, accidents happen. With sudden or accidental deaths, people not realizing they are dead can cause some energy to not move on to the next stage. Suicides, which are most often not reported in the media, can also be a cause of trapped energy. Many people who attempt suicide fail the first time, and so when death does claim them, it can be quite a while before the unfortunate soul realizes that it worked. Train stations have been a very popular place to die by suicide, as the act is generally over quickly and there's no one around to stop the victim. That is, of course, another reason why train stations are known for being haunted.

A woman described as a 1920s flapper has been spotted in the west corridor; she appears dancing, and then quickly fades away to nothing. The other ghost who seems to be a regular is that of a brakeman who was decapitated by a train in 1928. The brakeman appears on rainy nights with a lantern and waves it in warning at passing trains. Perhaps he fell onto the tracks or was caught in a deadly situation due to slipping in the rain.

The same anonymous security guard I spoke to also commented that all the other guides and staff who are there virtually alone in the evenings or very early mornings have heard the sound of footsteps; they are clearly heard but never seem to be connected to anything that can be seen. Interestingly enough, some of them seem to be rushing, while others go at a more regular pace. Even in the afterlife, some people are still in a hurry.

Many of the ghosts, says my security guard friend, appear as real as you or me. He claims they are simply people, for the most part, still trying to get to wherever they are going; they just seem to endlessly pass through the station.

My own experiences in the station are limited; my intuition is not strong enough to pick out a specific energy in a crowded location. I've been to parties in reputed haunted places, but unless I'm able to get away from all the other people, I can't seem to isolate any one feeling or energy. It makes sense: I'm overloaded by everyone else's energy bouncing all over the room, which makes it harder to pick up on an energy that may be limited or even diminished by time.

And so the river flows on between life and death, with the living unaware when someone on the other side of the veil shares their space as they rush to get where they're going. The next time you're in Waterfront Station, pause and take a look around. Is the person behind you on the escalator really there, or are you merely seeing a reflection of someone who was in the same space a long time ago? If you're there late at night, you may get a strong sense for the reality of another existence, and you may even encounter an entity that has no idea they've missed the last train to get where they needed to go.

PARK ROYAL SHOPPING CENTRE

P ARK ROYAL SHOPPING CENTRE, BUILT ON SQUAMISH NATION land, opened as Canada's first enclosed shopping centre in the fall of 1950. The mall was originally built to provide services to the nearby upscale British Properties, a neighbourhood designed with the wealthy in mind, so the mall has always tried to be upscale in terms of the goods and services it provides. The mall property currently occupies over 1.4 million square feet, with over 280 shops and services. It's a big place.

On a podcast that I co-hosted for three years, I asked people in Vancouver to share their ghost stories with me, and one of the listeners, Lisa Hemmerle, responded. Throughout the 1990s and into the 2000s, she worked at the Park Royal Shopping Centre, in various stores and areas on site. I was surprised—shopping centres hadn't been on my radar as far as ghost stories went, and I don't usually think of them as places where ghosts would hang out. But once I started doing a little research, it made sense that they could. I met with Lisa and her husband Thomas to hear their stories. They were both bright, funny, and engaging, and without a doubt they had stories to tell.

"Over the '90s and 2000s," says Lisa, "I worked at many different stores in Park Royal, which seems to be super haunted, but nobody talks about it. I didn't have paranormal experiences in every store I worked in, but I did have many encounters. Let me tell you about some of the experiences that really stand out in my memory."

AN UNSEEN CUSTOMER AFTER CLOSING TIME

I **WAS WORKING IN A TOY STORE AFTER CLOSING HOURS, AND** my co-worker was taking the garbage out while I was closing out the till. All the stores around us had locked their gates, and the staff had gone home, leaving us in a nook with no one around. Focused on counting the cash in the till, I heard a woman cough gently; then, in a clear voice with a British accent, she said, 'Excuse me, can you help me?'

"The voice was loud enough that I assumed the person was just outside the gate of the store, so I put the till back in the cash register, locked it, and went to the front gate to see who needed help. But there was no one there.

"At that moment, my co-worker appeared back from the garbage run. I asked her if she had seen the British woman looking for help. She looked at me like I was losing my mind. 'There's no one in the mall—you know that,' she said. I said I had clearly heard someone and that she sounded confused and older. 'Maybe we should look for her,' I said. 'She may have been locked in the mall after closing.' But my co-worker insisted there was no one in the mall and said I should count the till so we could close up and get the heck home. I did as she said and left the store without further incident; there was no trace of the unknown woman.

"While working at this toy store, the staff often had to go to the underground level, under the main floor of the mall, to store items in an area that reminded me of catacombs. The access to this area is via two old-fashioned cargo elevators with gates through which you can see the walls go by. The first time I rode in these I found it a bit thrilling, but I soon realized it was only a typical elevator. Of the two elevators, one of them was a perfectly comfortable place to be in, but the other was cold and anxiety-inducing. I mentioned to a peer that I disliked being in one of the elevators and she asserted it was haunted. 'Great, you're telling me this just as I'm about to go down with a load of toys,' I said.

"Shortly after, as I rode down the spooky elevator alone, something touched my shoulder. When I finished the delivery of toys to the storage area, I went back to the store and told my peer that she was right about the elevator. My shoulder was touched again on this elevator at other times, but only if I rode it alone."

NOTICE ME

"FOR OVER A DECADE I WORKED AT A BOOKSTORE, AND THE shelves had a slight incline, so the books were forced gently to the back of the shelf to prevent them from falling. But this didn't stop the books from falling off the shelves in Park Royal. Every morning, when we started our shift, our first duty was to walk all through the store and put all the books back on the shelves. Yet somehow the books never fell off during the day when the store was filled with staff and customers.

"During this time, the bookstore was my life—it was where I made friends and met my boyfriend (who would become my husband). So whenever I was asked to do something ridiculous, like wear a bookworm costume, I agreed without hesitation. I'd do anything for the job I loved.

"The day I wore the bookworm costume, my boyfriend and some of my co-workers came into work just to see me make a fool out of myself. This was a lot of fun, and later we were all in the crowded back room, where books upon books were stacked on their sides from floor to ceiling. We laughed about how sweaty I was and speculated about how many other sweaty people had worn the costume before me.

"While we were laughing, we all paused at the same time, and everyone's eyes went up to the ceiling. A mass market book had pulled itself off one of the towering stacks of books and was hovering in mid-air. The book then took a right turn and floated across the entire back room, then came to right beside where we were standing and fell. The book travelled over three metres in the shape of a capital L to get to us—again, I emphasize that this happened *in mid-air*.

"We stood there in silence for a moment, then we just started speaking again, talking about the next time I was to go out in the costume. But then I couldn't help myself—I had to ask: 'Hey, guys, was I the only person who saw that book float across the room?' The four people with me all agreed we had seen it, but the manager told us if we stopped working every time we saw a book float by, no work would get done. Strangely, we all agreed and got back to work. This was extraordinary, but I expect all booksellers have tales.

"Years later, that bookstore closed, and a skateboard and sports store moved in. One day I went in and chatted with the nice lady at the till there. 'So, how much of the stock do you find on the floor in the morning when your shifts start?' I asked. She stared at me as if I knew a secret I shouldn't. 'How?' was all she said. I told her that I'd worked in the bookstore that had previously been in this space, and that the stock had moved all the time. The girl went sheet white and said she'd thought it was all in her head."

CHEESE, PLEASE

"**A** GIANT HIGH-END GROCERY STORE WENT INTO PARK Royal Village, and I applied for a job in their cheese department. I hoped for a mundane, non-haunted work setting, as all my other haunted experiences were in the south mall building. I was hired, but within my first week of work my hopes for normalcy were dashed as my husband watched a glass container of milk pull itself out of the dairy fridge, hover, and then crash to the floor. One of the staff came running out with a mop and cleaned it up as my husband protested that he didn't drop it, saying he had no idea how the milk had fallen. The staff member told him this happened all the time and that he shouldn't worry about it.

"It may sound obvious, but cheese is incredibly heavy; a wheel of Parmesan alone is sixty pounds. When the department staff pushed cheese around on our carts, we would have hundreds of pounds of weight on it; the carts would roll, but they needed a real good push to go. It didn't take long for this cheese cart to go out of its way to gently bump me on my backside. During any closing shift that I was by myself, the cart would roll out of its way to gently hit me. By this time I suspected these bumps weren't accidental; I was getting bumped almost daily, and I was getting frustrated. I was also concerned it would start bumping me when I was on the meat slicer and that would be dangerous, and quite honestly I was working and didn't have time for any ghost's paranormal bullshit. Thankfully I got a chance to deal with it.

"I was sent to our cheese storage fridge to collect a day's worth of product. To get to the fridge I had to go through two doors; one closed me into a small room where I could see everyone coming and going. I was already wary of the cart hitting me, so when I was in the fridge loading it I put the back wheels in the drain well. This parked the cart so it couldn't move at all. I was by myself, looking between shelves for an elusive box, when the heavily loaded cart shot out of the drain well, rolling a metre forward and smacking me hard in the rear end, making me whack my head on the shelf. Thank goodness no co-workers were around because I dropped my guard and started yelling. 'Yeah, yeah, so you're a ghost—and, yes, I know you're here! Can't you see I'm working? What the hell can I do for you? Until you are paying me to help you, piss off!' This was unlike me on many levels, but I meant it, and it worked.

"Afterwards, I felt a bit guilty about yelling like that because I knew these were just spirits desperate to be noticed; they didn't seem dark like the ones in other areas of the mall. But as far I was concerned, it wasn't my circus, and those spirits were not my monkeys."

MY OWN EXPERIENCE in Park Royal Shopping Centre was a bit bizarre. Even though it was a quiet day at the mall, it felt crowded, and I felt like there were other indefinable things going on around me. One thing I experienced was in a new bookstore that had opened up close to where Lisa's original bookstore had been located. On Lisa's recommendation I headed for a certain section near the back of the store, and there was definitely a resident *something* there. But what was most striking about the bookstore was that when I left and walked back into the mall, it was like a record speeding up and the music returning to its normal pace—really bizarre. Until I'd left the bookstore, I wasn't even aware that things had slowed down so much while I was there. It was the strangest feeling.

When I mentioned this to Lisa, she said she could relate; in fact, both Lisa and her husband Thomas had experienced the same thing.

Do I think the Park Royal Shopping Centre is haunted? All I can say is that I certainly felt something paranormal there. Given Lisa's and Thomas's first-hand experiences there, along with those of countless other employees, I think it's a known thing. It's still a great mall—it has a nice vibe and lots of great stores. I would go back, no doubt. But would I want to spend a night in there? No. No, I would not.

HYCROFT MANOR

YCROFT MANOR, CONSTRUCTED BETWEEN 1909 AND 1911, is considered by some to be the most haunted house in Vancouver. The architect of this three-storey mansion was Thomas Hooper, who was very much in demand at the time. In fact, he is associated with a number of haunted buildings in Victoria, and when doing the Ghostly Walks there, we refer to Hooper as "the haunted architect."

There are rumours and theories. One of the grisliest is that Mr. Hooper belonged to a school of dark architectural beliefs, in London, England, where he got his start. This group believed that every building needed to have a resident soul if it was to be successful. And so for each project, it was ensured that someone would join the building crew who was perhaps older, of ill health, new to the country, or otherwise vulnerable and unlikely to be missed, ie. whose death would not be seen as mysterious or suspicious. This poor individual would eventually meet with an accident on the job site, resulting in their demise, or perhaps they would simply not show up to work one day. Either way, the building would get its soul, and Thomas Hooper went from one success to another in his architectural career. Hooper eventually died in 1935 at the age of seventy-seven and is now known as one of the most prolific architects of British Columbia's pioneer era.

Hycroft now appears to have at least seven resident ghosts who are pretty regular in their activities, even though the manor is no longer a private dwelling; since 1962, it has been home to the University Women's Club of Vancouver.

Originally built for businessman, general, and senator Alexander Duncan McRae, his first wife Blaunche, and their three daughters, the construction of the massive, thirty-room home cost just over $110,000 dollars (the equivalent of $3.3 million today). Built on 5.6 acres in the upscale Shaughnessy neighbourhood, it was set on the brow of a hill with an ocean and mountain view. The grounds also included a swimming pool, tea house, play house for the girls, and a coach house; the landscaping included an Italian garden and a rose garden. If the house itself were not impressive enough to make it an object of fascination and envy—it was, after all, considered one of Vancouver's premier homes—the parties and their reputation would have elevated its status. Huge, lavish events were held at Hycroft from the time it was built until the early 1940s. You weren't anybody in the Vancouver social scene until you'd been invited to a Hycroft party.

The McRaes lived—and partied—in the home until 1942 when Alexander "sold," or rather donated, the home to the federal government for the sum of $1.00, to use as a veteran's convalescent hospital. Mrs. McRae died that year, in a suite in the Hotel Vancouver, after leaving the home; Mr. McRae himself died four years later in Ottawa. Hycroft served as a veteran's hospital for eighteen years, and then was left vacant for two years, during which time plant life and some high-living racoons made their way inside. In 1962, the property was acquired by the University Women's Club of Vancouver.

It took the UWCV five years to bring the house and gardens back to their former glory, and to this day the club sees itself as the manor's guardian. The home has retained its original appearance and beauty—a rare feat for a house this age, especially in Vancouver. Most houses of this nature were either chopped up into apartments or seniors' homes, or simply levelled and the land sold for development.

The number and frequency of visits by the resident ghosts is yet another thing that sets Hycroft Manor apart. Of the seven identifiable ghosts who have taken up residence in the thirty-room house, Alexander and Blaunche McRae are among them, naturally. (By "identifiable," I mean that they are separate entities with their own characteristics, not that we know who all of these ghosts were when they were living.)

There have been many reports of an older man in a military uniform, seen all over the house. Bearing in mind that this building was used as a military hospital, complete with a morgue, this ghost's rather advanced age indicates that Alexander returns often to check on his former home. (It's safe to conclude this as there were no older men who had been wounded in war who would have been sent to this particular hospital to recover.) Does McRae linger in the home to check the many secret panels to make sure they are still intact and that he's able to still use them to hide his valuables?

His wife Blaunche is more of an "occasion" ghost, seen most often during celebrations and other special events, such as weddings, which are held on site. It is reported that one bride was concerned that an uninvited guest was lurking around. When she finally had a moment to bring this to the attention of one of the staff, she was asked to describe the mystery guest so they could be on the lookout. The bride saw the change that came over the staff member's face as she described the older woman that kept showing up around the room. The bride asked what was wrong, and that's when the staff member said that the guest she kept seeing was not actually alive and was certainly not a threat to the table count or open bar bill. The ghost of Blaunche McRae still loves the parties held in her home; the bigger the party, the more likely she is to show up, which makes sense as she was known throughout the city as the premier hostess of her time. One has to wonder if she compares the success of the festivities to those of her own, held so long ago.

The other ghosts include three former veterans who are nicknamed the pranksters—most likely veterans who stayed in the building when it was a military hospital. They've been known to tap people on the back, cause chills, and shut doors while also making the sound of footsteps all over the twenty-thousand-square-foot property.

Another ghost is the former head nurse, who seems to prefer to remain around the former bedrooms. This makes sense as she would be checking on her former charges, even though they are long departed. Witnesses have seen her appear as a mist or fog; she has even been caught in this form by film crews for the television shows filmed in Hycroft, such as *The X Files*. The final ghost is simply known only as the "weeping man" because of the sounds of a man crying, as heard in the ballroom.

As haunted as it is, I found Hycroft Manor to be a warm, welcoming place. Perhaps the party-loving spirits of the departed owners are still happy to welcome people to their home. Maybe it's the head nurse who dedicated her life to caring for others. Or it could be the energy, passion, and kindness of the people of the University Women's Club. In any case, it's a beautiful property, and it doesn't have a creepy haunted house vibe at all.

Hycroft Manor has already had a full and storied existence, and thanks to the wonderful women of the UWCV, it will continue to be an elegant treasure for the City of Vancouver. While it may no longer be home to any living people, it certainly continues to be home to some substantial spirits.

UNIVERSITY OF BRITISH COLUMBIA

ONE STORY I'VE HEARD REPEATEDLY IN EVERY REGION OF Canada where I've lived is the one about the disappearing hitchhiker. You've most likely heard it before, too. It usually involves someone driving alone along a lonely stretch of road, where they either pull over to pick up a woman or a woman appears in their backseat. If asked where she wants to go or where she's headed, she tells the driver. At some point in the journey, before the driver can reach the destination, the young woman vanishes. This is often linked to a car accident or pedestrian fatality that occurred somewhere along that stretch of road at some point in the past. See? I told you you'd heard it before. However, the story I'm about to tell you is a little different.

Lydia Williams, owner of Ghostly Vancouver Tours, shared this part of the story with me, and I was so excited to finally have a hitchhiker story with some verifiable details. Lydia first heard it many years ago from someone very close to the family, and she was gracious enough to pass it on to me.

THE STORY OF SUSAN JONES

OUR HITCHHIKER, A UNIVERSITY OF BRITISH COLUMBIA student in 1965, has a name: Susan Jones. On the night of her demise, Susan had spent the evening in the UBC library. Described as a pretty girl with long blond hair, Susan had a boyfriend who was due to pick her up later that night to drive her home.

Susan's boyfriend arrived at the library to drive her home, but unfortunately, he was drunk. After she got in the car, he began driving quite a bit faster than the recommended speed limit. Susan asked him to slow down, but being an impulsive young man in his early twenties and quite drunk, he ignored her. The inevitable took place, just past St. Anselm's Anglican church, where he lost control of the car and slammed into a tree. Susan was killed instantly, but her boyfriend survived. The tree still bears the scar of the impact, almost as a silent memorial for the young woman whose life was cut short.

After this tragedy, people went back to their lives, but stories soon began to crop up. However, they weren't the typical stories of young men who swore up and down that they'd picked up a pretty blond woman on University Boulevard who had then disappeared. There was more.

Susan's devastated parents experienced further distress from an occurrence that took place at least once a week. There would be a knock at their door, usually quite late at night, and when they answered they would find a confused young man who wanted to know if a young blond woman lived there. Why would these guys be coming to Susan's old home? All of them told the same story: They were driving down University Boulevard and saw a young blond woman hitchhiking along the side of the road near the church. Naturally they'd stop—it was dark out, and in 1965 it wasn't proper for a young lady to be wandering around in the dark. They'd ask her where she was heading, and she would give them her old home address where she'd lived with her parents until her death. Of course, before these young men could get her home, the young woman would simply vanish. This is why the men were coming to the house—they wanted to know what was going on.

Did they really see what they thought they saw? Did it happen? Was there some other proof to be found at the home address they'd been given? Unfortunately for Susan's parents, they were now in the horrible position of having to explain over and over again that their daughter had been killed on that stretch of road, and that she was buried, and that there was no way she could be hitchhiking. How awful for them.

These nocturnal visits continued with distressing regularity, and finally Susan's parents turned to their local Catholic priest for help. When they explained what was going on, he agreed to help them, but he admitted that he didn't know a lot about this field of spiritual practice. The good news was his friend, an Anglican priest, was trained in this area, and he asked Susan's parents if he could invite the other priest to assist in the situation. Susan's parents, desperate for a solution, agreed.

A tiny group of them went one evening to the location where Susan had died a few months earlier. The group included Susan's parents, her younger sister, Mary, and the two priests. They laid a wreath at the tree, and the priests said some prayers, sprinkled some holy water, and generally tried to bring peace to Susan's spirit while at the same time sending her on her way.

It didn't work. The stories persisted, and the visits from confused young men continued. Finally, after a year or so, Susan's parents were forced to sell the house and move. They could no longer endure the constant reminders of their lost daughter who seemed desperately to want to come home.

The stories of a pretty young blond hitchhiker continue to this day. She gives the driver an address and then simply vanishes before the destination has been reached. Susan is not seen as often, but she is not forgotten: In 2015, the fiftieth anniversary of the death, flowers were left by the tree with a note that read: *Jonesy, I am sorry.*

The paranormal aspect of Susan's story must have had a profound impact on Susan's sister, Mary. When she grew up, Lydia tells me, she became a nun.

I VISITED THE tree near the church on a quiet weekend afternoon. There were not a lot of people around, and the area had a feeling of sadness to it. I don't know if the energy is as strong as it was fifty years ago, but there certainly seems to be some residual sadness in that area. How many people waiting for a bus there at night sense it? Do they feel as if someone is with them, or do they simply feel a little uncomfortable and look hopefully up the road for the reassuring lights of an approaching bus?

The spirit of Susan Jones is still reliving her final night, and while she is not spotted as often, she has not been forgotten, even if her story can sometimes get lost in urban legends and folklore. Sometimes, if we're willing to dig a bit deeper, we find that these legends come from a place of truth.

A PRIVATE HOME IN KERRISDALE

"**A** DOCTOR HAD THIS HOME BUILT," SAID THE CURRENT homeowner as she walked me through the impressive front door and into the grand entrance hall. The feeling or "spidey-sense" I've mentioned before descended on my shoulders like a wet, heavy blanket. I felt my back tense, and I fought the urge to look around furtively. It had been a long time since I'd had that strong a reaction to a building; as it turned out, my sense was not wrong.

This particular home and homeowner will remain anonymous at their request; the neighbourhood is not the kind that would readily accept that a local home is haunted. Nevertheless, this house has a history, and this homeowner had a story to tell.

Let's call the homeowner Kate. According to Kate, everything started out fine when she and her husband moved into the home after the birth of their first child. They were looking forward to growing their family and having a big, beautiful house in which to make that dream come true.

For the first year and a half, Kate pretty much left the house as is. It wasn't until 1990 that she felt ready to make some changes. Becoming a new mom had taken a lot of her energy and time, and she just couldn't face taking on the rather imposing project of redoing this very large, very old house. The previous owners had not updated anything since the late 1970s, and so it was in dire need of a facelift. But these were not her initial concerns when moving in.

Odd things that had taken place here and there, but when Kate shared concerns or even mentioned anything of this nature to her husband, he would scoff and tell her she needed to get out of the house more. His other standard line was that it was an old house and that houses settle and make noises depending on the outside temperature and other factors. These explanations annoyed Kate as she felt she was being condescended to, but she had nothing to add other than her own experiences in this house—specifically that she never really felt alone there.

The first thing she'd noticed was the sound of footsteps—soft footfalls, most likely of a woman, could be heard in different parts of the house at different times of the day and night. They did not seem to have a pattern or set time, they were just . . . there. Kate would notice them most often when she was rocking her baby to sleep, or had sat down after completing some chore, or when she'd pick up the book she was currently reading. Anything that required her to be quiet and still seemed to be the trigger. The sounds didn't alarm her, but they were noticeable—and they were not the sounds of a house settling.

After a few months, the sounds grew in variety. Now, from time to time—not as often as the footfalls—there was the soft sound of closing doors. By this time Kate could tell the difference between some of the doors by a particular creak or a whoosh as it dragged across carpet; it was often the same two or three doors that she would hear open and softly close.

Unlike in many of these stories, the baby was never affected. You often hear about babies and young children reacting or even interacting with whatever energy is there, but Kate said that would have been a dealbreaker for her if it had tried to connect with her child. This spirit must have known that, for there was never any evidence that it had paid attention to Kate's baby. Kate feels the spirit must have known this or at least felt it was a line to not cross.

At this point, soon after moving in, these were the only

interruptions, and Kate seemed to be the only one who could hear them. It did make her feel a bit uncomfortable but not enough to diminish her love for the house or make her feel that this was not her home. Kate simply accepted that something else was there, and as long as they could co-exist, she was fine with that.

Then things changed.

Soon Kate had more confidence, time, and energy, and she decided it was time to change up the house to make it more her style and to make it a place where the family could grow. These changes would include putting in an ensuite bathroom in the master bedroom, knocking down some walls on the lower level, and generally bringing the old place up to date both in décor as well as the wiring and other systems. It was an extensive and expensive job, and Kate was determined to take care of it all.

Being her own general contractor was, at times, overwhelming as Kate learned the ins and outs of getting the right tradespeople in at the right times and how much one person ending on time mattered to the whole process. One misstep in timing would create a domino effect that would throw off the whole project.

Only a quarter of the way into the massive job, Kate discovered she was pregnant with her second child, and so the need to get this renovation done quickly and efficiently was even more important. However, that didn't seem likely given what had started to happen.

Kate couldn't retain tradespeople; they were quitting, and doing so quickly. Some of them would tell her why; others would just be gone when she would return from an errand and wouldn't take her calls. The reason? Ghosts—at least those willing to talk about it named it as such. But Kate was sure her house did not have a previous reputation for being haunted. She had met all the neighbours and hinted around such a possibility, but no one had mentioned anything (usually there's someone who will). When the tradespeople expanded on their stories, Kate understood why they were leaving as fast as she could hire them.

These grown men—as all of the tradespeople happened to be—were being harassed in different ways, but to great effect. Battery-powered tools had their power packs drained with no warning, and they no longer worked. Plug-in tools were unplugged, not just once, but multiple times and often with the plug end lying in the middle of the room, to make it clear that it hadn't just fallen out of the outlet. These poor guys were tapped on the shoulder, then, turning around, expecting to see their coworkers, they discovered no one there. Some heard their names called by a woman, and assuming it was Kate they would head to where they'd heard the voice, only to discover the house was empty.

One plumber was determined to not be frightened away from the job; he had worked in haunted locations before and none of this got to him. However, when the spirit decided to undo an entire day's work from the day before—the pipes were lying on the floor as if awaiting installation, something the plumber had spent a good six hours doing already—he quit, apologized to Kate, and added, "Good luck, lady!"

By this time, the ghost was no longer walking demurely through the halls and softly closing doors—now it was regularly stomping around the house and slamming doors. It was obviously upset, but the ghost wasn't the only one upset; Kate herself was getting frustrated and exasperated. At this point she had to have the renovation done before the second baby came. It was bad enough that the three of them were living in a construction zone, even if it was manageable, but it would not be okay with another baby as well. The problem was that this was Kate's first experience with anything paranormal, and she was not sure exactly what to do. But in the end, Kate's temper saved the day—and the renovation.

After spending the day trying to find another plumber, electrician, and drywaller, with vague promises from each that they would try to find time to stop by to look at the job, Kate had gone out for groceries. The toddler was at a neighbour's place; Kate had left her there so she could be quicker about the shopping and get home, then go get the child once dinner was started. After she pulled into her driveway, she gathered the bags of groceries and hip-checked her way through the back door and into the kitchen. She stopped dead in her tracks. Every cupboard door was open, and every single drawer was pulled out almost to the tipping point. At that point, Kate says, she just lost it. She slammed the groceries on the centre island and yelled out loud:

"Enough! Enough of this! We have to change the house to make it work for us! We've always got along in the past, and I know you don't like this, but if you keep it up we'll just leave, and who knows who you will get in here then. So stop it! Leave the workmen alone, and just *stop* it!"

With that, she whirled around, leaving the groceries on the counter, and out the back door, which she slammed behind her. Kate then went into the driveway to cool off and figured she'd better go get her daughter from the neighbour's house. She reflected that it was like she'd just yelled at a roommate, and though she felt a bit foolish, she also realized she had got out some of the frustration that had been simmering, so there was some relief there too.

Kate brought her daughter home, closed every cupboard, shut every drawer, put the groceries away, and began making dinner. Not knowing what to expect from the spirit, she told her husband what had happened. This time, thankfully, he had no explanation for what Kate had witnessed, so he remained silent on the whole thing. When they went to bed, nothing was heard throughout the night at all. Perhaps something had changed.

The next day, by some miracle, all three of the tradespeople showed up and accepted the work that had been started but not completed. None of those three, nor any subsequent workers, left before the job was done, and no one had any comments about the house. Yes, something *had* changed!

The day the last painter left was a relief for Kate, for so many reasons. Her dream renovation was complete, but most importantly they had a beautiful, safe place for their new baby. It was only when Kate was sitting alone, her daughter upstairs having a nap, that she heard soft footfalls go up the stairs; then there was the quiet noise of a door being gently opened and closed. That was the moment Kate realized that whatever shared her house was back, and more importantly, it was behaving itself. At this point she decided to welcome it. She recognized that her outburst had saved not only the renovation, but her love of the house—and even, perhaps a little bit, her fondness for the spirit that shared it with them.

NOW, MANY YEARS later, we were seated in the living room. Kate had made tea for us, and there was no doubt we were not alone. In fact, as we sat there, it almost felt as if a woman had joined us. The woman felt very upper class, very refined, and while she certainly knew how to behave in polite society, she was a woman used to getting her own way and not tolerating fools. The story and her interactions with Kate and the workmen made perfect sense. I could feel that she liked and approved of Kate. My guess is that she simply, like most spirits, did not like change or alteration to her environment. Kate had put her in her place, and she respected that.

As we sat sipping our tea, Kate mused on the past and said that whatever was around back then was most definitely still around. I asked her if she had ever wanted the spirit gone, or considered having someone come in to get rid of it. Kate smiled. "Oh no, now that the kids have moved out, I know when I hear it, and it reminds me that I'm never alone here. It's a comfort." With a little laugh, she added, "But heaven help the next owner if they decide to renovate."

THE ROYAL CROWN CASTLE
RESTAURANT AND BAR

N 1878, NOBODY COULD HAVE PREDICTED THE SITE WOULD one day hold the Royal Crown Castle Restaurant and Bar—and a daycare wasn't in the plans either.

Overlooking the Fraser River in New Westminster, the site was a popular and strategic one. The Squamish people used it as a camp because of its elevation, giving one the ability to see for long distances up and down the river; then, for a time, it was used as a military camp. At one point, while New Westminster and Victoria competed for designation as the capital city of the Colony of British Columbia, the building site showcased the province's first colonial Government House.

Even today, it does indeed resemble a castle, which makes sense as it was designed and built with a single purpose: to give British Columbia a place to house its maximum-security prisoners rather than have them shipped east to places like Kingston.

From 1878 to 1980, the British Columbia Penitentiary resided on this site, and the structure that is currently known as the Royal Crown Castle Restaurant is in the building that had formerly been the gatehouse to the much larger penitentiary; it was part of a complex that once was the roughest, most dangerous prison in Canada until it closed in 1980. Of the complex, only four pieces remain: the gatehouse, the coal house, the storage shed, and an over-grown and mostly forgotten prisoner graveyard.

Back in the day, prisoners would be shipped up the Fraser River to the penitentiary's dock; then they would be unloaded and taken through a tunnel to the gatehouse, where they would be processed. These days the tunnel shed is used for storage, but I imagine back when prisoners were transferred there from boats it would have been a terrifying place to be brought to.

For many men, BC Pen, as it came to be known, was truly a place of no return; only the worst prisoners were brought here.

There is a long history of prisons being haunted, and this makes a lot of sense. Energy-wise, there is so much negativity here, so much anger, regret, hatred, fear. Many men died within the prison walls either in riots or by murder or simply running out of time; certainly, being in prison would have hastened that time. There's such an intense history that many old prisons are now open for tours and routinely put on ghost investigations, allowing paranormal groups to come in to see what they can experience. The Royal Crown Castle (now closed indefinitely in this COVID-19 era) is no exception; they generously offered Paul Busch and his Greater-Vancouver-based paranormal group Cornerstone Supernatural the chance to investigate.

There are three levels to the building: basement, main floor, and second floor. The establishment has a public bar and restaurant area and a private, rentable room known as the "white room." The first presence Cornerstone came across was one that was familiar to staff and some sensitive customers. Of the seven spirits that were sensed here by the group's mediums, the one in the bar was one of the most popular. The energy would sit at the bar and seemed to watch everything going on. There is a definite, measurable cold spot in the area where this energy is sensed. I wonder what it will get up to now that the bar is closed.

When the group went into the white room, their K2 meters (devices that light up when they sense electrical energy) went crazy, though there didn't seem to be any clear reason for it during the investigation. However, when the restaurant was still open, one of the staff members said she hated being in that room by herself, usually when she had to set up or dismantle tables and chairs for a private event. Any time she could, she tried to work with someone else or talk someone else into working with her. The only way she could describe the feeling in that room was that it was as if someone very, very angry was watching her and resenting her presence.

On the upper level, two figures were frequently sighted, nicknamed "the tall" and "the small." They interacted with investigators—sometimes audibly, such as with a knock on the wall, or visually by using the SLS device, which plots points of energy. On that device, "the small" was shown raising its hand and waving. "The small" has often been reported as the source of odd noises in the building; there was often the sound of someone walking around on the upper level, even when the place was empty, prior to opening, or when all staff were accounted for, with everyone downstairs. Staff grew accustomed to ignoring it all together and decided to leave whatever was up there to do its thing. Other areas on this upper floor had a lot of K2 activity that couldn't be explained by wiring or anything else electrical.

The basement level, the most disturbing, contained cells where prisoners would have been placed while waiting for processing. In four or five of the cells there was K2 activity that had no business being there—almost as if the ghosts had felt compelled to return to perpetually endure what was probably the most traumatic experience of their lives. The energy down there was heavy, dark, angry, and very negative. Lots of activity was going on around the investigators, with sounds and "corner of the eye phenomena." No one, living or otherwise, felt very happy down there.

One of the investigators was physically shoved where he was standing, as if to move him out of the way; indeed, the doorway he'd been standing in would have been very busy with guards taking prisoners from the cells in the basement to the first floor, where they would have been processed. It felt to him as if something had shouted, "Get out of the way!" and then given him a push. The investigator actually had marks on his body at the point of impact.

The cemetery is the last original feature of this once-sprawling property; it's now hidden away, surrounded by houses and condominium buildings. If you can find your way in there, you'll find forty-eight mostly hidden, mostly buried markers. This doesn't even fully represent who exactly is buried there, for not everyone got a marker. The cemetery was used from 1913 until the last interment in 1968, a final resting place for the prisoners that no one claimed. Many of them died by their own hand, and by all accounts it's a sad and desolate place. It's almost as if the municipality, now the official owner of the land, would rather have forgotten about this place, perhaps in the same way many of these men were forgotten in life. Only recently, in 2018, the city cleaned up the cemetery and posted signage to share what it is and what it means to the history of the community. Shadow figures have been seen here, especially late in the day or in the early morning. I doubt much rest was found in a place like this. At least now the graves are being cared for.

The former gatehouse for the BC Penitentiary is undoubtedly a place of spirits—and hopefully it will once again be a place of good food, good drinks, and fun evenings out. But for now, at least at night, it remains devoid of the living. The spirits of the dead are free to roam, do as they wish, and go where they like; perhaps it's a small comfort to think that in death these ghosts are getting to do in this place what they could never have done alive.

SHARED SPACES

MOST OF US HAVE LIVED IN A SHARED SPACE AT ONE TIME or another. These spaces can take many forms—the ubiquitous basement suite, a roommate situation, or even a cool downtown apartment. Apartments are great for low-commitment accommodation in which you only have to worry about your own four walls. Most of the time there's no garden or garage to fuss over—just walk through the front door, through the lobby, and into your own little piece of the city. For some, an apartment is just what they want, and they stay for a lifetime; others move on, either to own a different kind of shared space, like a downtown condominium—I think Vancouver has a few of those—or out of the downtown area altogether so that by moving farther away they can eventually afford to buy a house.

All this convenience and low-maintenance living comes at a price. Much like hospitals, hotels, and theatres, you have not only a high rate of turnover, but you also have people taking ownership (at least in their minds) of "their" space. So when it's time to leave, some people seem to find it hard to let go, especially if they don't know they're being forced to leave. Whether they know they're gone or not, many of them have a way of ensuring they're noticed and acknowledged.

AN UNEXPECTED ROOMMATE

JUST OFF GRANVILLE STREET NEAR WEST 15TH AVENUE, there is plenty of rentable accommodation. One of these was very innocently moved into by a man named Jason. Having just acquired a new job that meant relocating to Vancouver from his hometown of Edmonton, Jason was excited to start his new life and wanted to be close enough to downtown that he could explore the city relatively easily via public transportation.

Jason moved into his new apartment on a beautiful day in June. The apartment itself was in an older building most likely built in the 1930s, but it was well taken care of and full of light. A handsome brick frontage and neatly kept lawn were also part of its charm, not to mention it only had three storeys. The apartment had a simple layout: two bedrooms, one bathroom, and a living room with a kitchen on the other side.

Jason's first night in his new apartment went smoothly, even if he was utterly exhausted from the move, both physically and mentally. Once the bed was set up, he collapsed onto it and didn't wake up until the sun was shining in his face the next morning. He spent the rest of that morning putting things away and getting the place straightened out. It didn't take long; he didn't have much stuff as he'd moved directly to Vancouver after graduating from university, where he'd lived in a crowded shared accommodation situation.

As Jason had moved in on a Friday and didn't start work till Monday, he had two whole days to get to know his neighbourhood. So he ventured out and found the local grocery store, drugstore, and, most importantly, the pub. He returned from his adventures tired, but he was happy and not in the same state of exhaustion as the night before. He headed for bed and fell asleep quickly.

At around 2:00 AM Jason woke up. He assumed it was because his bladder was protesting the beers he'd consumed earlier. He headed for the bathroom, did what he had to do, and then headed back to the bedroom. On his way back to bed, he noticed the light was on in the living room. Odd, he thought; he was sure he'd turned everything off when he went to bed earlier. He trudged into the living room to shut off the light and realized it wasn't a light, it was the television. That was even stranger; Jason knew he had not turned it on even once since he moved in, other than to quickly check that the cable was working. He went in, grabbed the remote, turned off the television, and went back to bed.

In the morning, he got up, grabbed a shower, had some coffee, and figured he would see what was on TV. Turning it on, he slumped back on the couch and, just as he was settled, he heard the bathroom door moving. He already knew it creaked quite loudly—he had thought about going to the hardware store to grab some oil to get it to shut up—but that was not what was on his mind at the moment. The creaking of the door sounded as if someone was standing there, moving it open and closed, slowly and repeatedly. Jason got up, wandered over to the other side of the apartment, and saw that nothing was moving and no one was there.

After this incident, he began to realize the TV had not been on by mistake. Jason had grown up in a home that was open to whatever was going on, ghost-wise, and he figured that whether he liked it or not, he was stuck with a roommate again—only this one wasn't going to help out with the rent.

Jason grew accustomed to coming home and finding windows open that had been left closed; sometimes lights or the TV were turned on, which was nice to come home to (Jason said it made him feel less lonely). The only thing that bothered him was being woken up in the middle of the night to hear the other bedroom door click shut or open and the bathroom door creaking—he never did get the oil to fix it. It wasn't the creepiness of the activity that annoyed him; it was the inconvenience of being woken up. When it came to everything else, Jason says, he got used to it. Sometimes the cupboard doors in the kitchen would be open, drawers pulled out, but nothing dangerous ever happened. No water was left running, and the stove was never left on. To Jason, it was like having a quiet, low-key, introverted roommate, and he was okay with it. Jason never tried to communicate with it; he was remarkably easygoing about having it around. When he left the apartment a few years later to move in with a new girlfriend, he did say goodbye to the empty place.

Jason is a pretty laid-back guy—not just when it comes to the paranormal, but toward life in general. It can be a different story when two people of contrasting temperaments experience such phenomena.

COFFEE GHOSTS

LYDIA WILLIAMS, OWNER AND OPERATOR OF GHOSTLY Vancouver Tours, was not quite sure what was happening in her new condo when things started brewing. The building—built in 1971—wasn't new, but it wasn't that old either, and there were no renters; only owners were in the units. Many of them had been in the building since it was built, and so naturally there was more than one who passed away while living there. In Lydia's own words:

"I'm not a medium—I've never actually seen or conversed with a ghost—but I have felt them and smelled them, which has to be the least impressive of psychic abilities out there. We moved into our apartment in 2002, and the 'coffee ghost' started visiting around September 2007.

"I'm a night owl who doesn't drink coffee—ever; my husband is the one who drinks the stuff. I would stay up late, alone, watching television or reading in the living room, and would suddenly be hit by the strong scent of coffee. All the windows were always closed, so the smell couldn't be coming from the outside. I would even check the hallway of my building in case someone had walked by with a pot of coffee at two in the morning, but the scent lingered solely in the living room. It happened a few times, and only to me, before my parents visited one night.

"My dad and my husband had retired for the evening, but my mother and I stayed up late (we're both night owls) chatting in the living room. Again, I was hit by the coffee smell, but I didn't say anything. In the middle of a sentence, my mom stopped talking and said, "Do you smell coffee?" I was happy she smelled it too because part of me was worried I was having seizures. We both walked around my apartment and into the outside hallway, but again the scent remained in the living room. I asked my mom if there was a deceased family member who liked coffee. She said all of them did, pretty much; that didn't help me identify the source.

"A month or two later, I was watching *Ghost Hunters* early one night. In that episode, a bathroom tap had turned itself on for no reason that the investigation team was able to discover. I thought, *What would it be like if something just turned itself on in my apartment?* One second later, the coffee maker loudly started up. My husband came out from the den, and we both walked over to the kitchen to gawk at the appliance. Some folks have argued that we had set the timer accidentally. But the clock on the coffee maker had been blinking 12:00 for the last three years because we could never figure out how to set the time. My husband, who is both an avid coffee drinker and total skeptic, turned it off and chalked it up to random, non-paranormal weirdness.

"Not long after that, maybe a month later, I had a different experience, though I'm not sure I can attribute it to the coffee ghost. I was in the kitchen one morning, standing in front of the toaster, waiting for my toast. Out of the corner of my eye, I noticed a dishcloth swinging wildly where it hung on the oven handle. The stove is just a couple inches to the left of the toaster. I turned toward it and thought, *Huh, that's funny.* There is absolutely no way to get a draft through my galley kitchen in a condo with windows only on the opposite side, which were all shut that morning. Then I felt an entity pass through me. It's hard to describe the feeling of an energy going through you—it was more than just a sick feeling in the pit of my stomach. And it didn't last for more than a couple of seconds. At that point, I felt the ghost had crossed the line! I got angry and said something along the lines of, 'That's it, no more! Out!' And the coffee/kitchen ghost did not bother me again."

THE FARAWAY GHOST

THIS LAST APARTMENT STORY INVOLVES A FRIEND OF MINE and an odd experience we had over the phone.

Karen had just moved into a condo, as a roommate to the new owner. I spoke with Karen when she made her big move to Vancouver, while I was living in Winnipeg, and she reported that everything seemed to be normal; there was nothing unusual to report.

A few weeks went by, and then I got a call from Karen. It turned out to be one of the most bizarre phone conversations I've ever had—not so much because of what she said, but because of what I saw while we were talking. I have spoken before about what I call my "spidey sense" that seems to live in my brain—how I've never seen a ghost, but have had pictures from them sort of shoved into my head, like someone handing me a stack of photographs, and how from "looking" at them I'm able to figure out what's going on. This has not happened often—I certainly don't go looking for it—and if I'm in a haunted location, I usually have my guard up. However, if a friend needs help, I will always do whatever I can. This phone conversation turned out to be one of those times.

Karen was calling on behalf of herself and her roommate. Karen and I had some shared experiences of a paranormal nature from when we were in school together, so it made sense she would think of me at a time like this. As Karen described what was happening, I started to get the pictures, but they didn't seem to make much sense.

Karen said she and her roommate were having problems in the condo unit. They seemed to get locked in their rooms, as in the door handles simply wouldn't turn to allow them out. Sometimes water would start running randomly in the kitchen and the main bathroom, and they'd have to go shut it off. Most upsetting was that she and her roommate didn't feel safe in their own condominium as they felt as if a shadow man was lurking in the halls. They would hear heavy footfalls outside and be frightened enough to yell to each other from their rooms, "Do you hear that?" Sure enough, the other one always would. Lights would flicker for no reason, even after bulbs had been changed and wiring had been checked. In their bedrooms they felt safe; they spent most of their free time in their rooms, venturing out only when absolutely necessary. All of this was obviously upsetting to the new owner of the condo as well as to Karen, who had just moved in.

I had never been to the condo, nor did I know the address, so it struck both of us as odd when I began to get strong impressions and was able to not only accurately describe the layout of the condo, but also the view from the living room patio doors and balcony. "Yes," Karen said, "everything you're saying is all true." This really threw me. *How could this be?* I wondered. I was over two thousand kilometres away—how could I be picking up anything?

I asked Karen if there was a building manager, and indeed there was. I told her she needed to ask about the previous owner of the condo unit. I also told her that I saw an elderly gentleman in a recliner, wearing a brown suit. I could see him in my head, very clearly, and I could also see that he was dead. I even described where the recliner had been placed in the room: the corner, beside the sliding patio door in the living room. All of it was *right there*. It was one of the strangest things I'd ever experienced. And it was about to get a little stranger.

Karen had always loved going out, so it was a pretty regular routine for her and her new roommate to get dressed up on Friday and Saturday nights, head to the clubs, and dance the night away.

I knew this was a regular thing for Karen, but it never occurred to me that it might end up being a problem.

A few weeks later, Karen called me again. She had met the building manager and had asked about the previous owner. Turns out they had been friends. The building manager and the elderly former owner would have dinner every Sunday night, down in the manager's condo. One night, however, dinner was on the table, but the older man did not show up. The manager called him, but there was no answer. He went up and knocked on the door; again, no answer. So he used his building pass key and found his friend deceased, sitting in the recliner by the patio doors, dressed in a brown suit—the one he always wore to church. It looked like he'd got home and just sat down for a minute before changing out of his suit, only to never get up again. Of course, the building manager was upset, but he did what was needed to ensure his friend had a proper goodbye. Turns out the brown-suited fellow was very religious, very conservative, and had very clear on ideas on how young ladies should behave.

When I heard this, it suddenly all made sense. "I don't want to sound harsh," I said, "but I have to ask. When you two go to the clubs, you dress up in . . . well . . . club clothes, right?"

Karen laughed. "Of course we do," she said, "that's half the fun."

I let her know that she was going to have to find a way around that if she and her roommate wanted to live in the condo in peace. Why? The late tenant was possibly unaware that he was dead and was feeling responsible for the girls who had come to stay. In his own way, and in any way he could, he was trying to express to them his unhappiness with their actions. I asked Karen if the activity was worse on the weekends and she confirmed it was. During the week both women wore business attire, and when they came home they would routinely change into sweats and other relaxed clothing. Certainly not the outfits they were putting together to go to the clubs.

I called Karen a few weeks later to find out how things were going. She affirmed that since they took their club clothes to work with them on Fridays and got changed there, and would go to a girl-friend's house to get ready if they were going out again on Saturday night, things had definitely died down. The odd flickering of lights or the sound of light foot fall were all that were left of the disapproving old man, whose generational outlook had clashed terribly with the young women who now lived in what used to be his condo. The women were relieved that they could now live in the entirety of the space and not be confined to their bedrooms. Who knows, perhaps the old man even lightened up a bit.

It wasn't till almost twenty-five years later that someone who I respect very much explained to me how the whole event occurred. I could not understand how I was able to sense what I could while being so far away. My friend explained that energy knows no limits in terms of distance, and what I was connecting to wasn't so much the place, but to my friend Karen; it was my ability to connect with *her* that allowed me to connect with the space and the situation. It took a while, but I was happy to eventually get an answer.

When we share spaces with other people, we have to remember there may not just be living people present. People and energies have access to shared spaces, so it's best to respect everyone you come across, whether you see them in the hall, the laundry room, or at the end of your bed in the middle of the night. If they show up there, they might be the former tenants or owners of the space you now, if only temporarily, call your own.

VANCOUVER ART GALLERY

F YOU HAPPENED TO READ *VICTORIA'S MOST HAUNTED*, YOU'LL know the name Francis Mawson Rattenbury, the architect responsible for most of the notable buildings in Victoria's Inner Harbour. He lived a very colourful life, and after his demise he returned to haunt at least two of the notable buildings he built, including the Legislature buildings and the Empress Hotel.

Why do I bring him up? Well, Rattenbury was a busy and popular architect, and he was also responsible for the design of the British Columbia Provincial Court building in downtown Vancouver.

The building that now houses the Vancouver Art Gallery started out as the province's courthouse, from the time of its completion in 1911 until 1979, when its last case was heard. In 1983, the gallery took up residence, and while plans for a new building are in the works, the museum continues to operate out of this stately structure—and everything that comes with it. Believe me when I say there's a lot more that comes with this building than meets the eye.

Rumours about the building being haunted have long circulated. How could they not? It's a museum; history has shown, time and again, that it's standard for such institutions to be haunted. It makes sense: They are spotlight-lit places with shadowy edges, with objects collected from all over the world in many different circumstances that may or may not have energy attached, not to mention the sheer output of emotion invested in some of these works of art, either by the people who create them or through the response of those viewing them. All of these factors make for a formidable combination in terms of spirit or energy activity. In the same way, courthouses—filled with drama, joy, angst, terror, and fury—would leave an indelible mark on the spiritual atmosphere of any building that houses these trials that are necessary to keep society running.

So, putting an art gallery *in* a former court house? Double whammy! Indeed, this building, lovely as it is, does not disappoint when it comes to supernatural activity.

As I have said before, when writing a book of ghostly tales, one needs to interview two groups of people: night cleaners and security guards. Luckily for us, our stories involve both.

Speaking on condition of anonymity, two individuals told me about their time at the museum. It's worth noting that these are people who are not particularly sensitive to spiritual energy.

One of these individuals is a fellow named Dave. A man in his mid-sixties, he is exceptionally youthful in mindset and behaviour. He's open to new experiences, but he would never describe himself as a die-hard believer. Dave was a security guard in the building for many years before finally retiring three years ago. Willing to accept the unknown as just that, Dave had many encounters in the building and even tried to help solve some of the puzzling events that happened there.

Dave had been asked to figure out what was going on with the paperwork on people's desks, which was regularly getting messed up during off hours. Most offices have a standard policy that cleaners are never to touch the desks, for obvious reasons of confidentiality, and to generally avoid interfering with workspaces; the same policy applied to the cleaning crew at the gallery.

In spite of this, the desks in the offices close to the back entrance of the building were constantly left in disarray. Staff were nearly convinced someone was deliberately messing things up to throw them off their jobs, as some of the paperwork appeared to be almost hidden on the desk. Security staff had been asked to look into this, and Dave was one of those involved. There were no cameras in those offices, but there were on the entrances and exits of the building. The cameras revealed that even when some of the office staff left *after* the cleaning staff, the desks were still getting messed up, even though no one else had been in or out of those areas. It made no sense. Why would a ghost feel the need to mess up the paperwork on people's desks in an art gallery?

It turns out that, historically, this area is where the prisoners would have been led into the courthouse to be taken to the holding area on the day of their trials. Perhaps whatever was messing up the papers on the gallery employees' desks assumed it was interfering with the papers for court cases or trials, and thus creating a convenient delay in the proceedings. Regardless of the reason, the case was never solved, and the messy desk problem continues to this day. Most employees know to simply lock everything up in a drawer when leaving for the night to avoid the problem altogether.

Dave also shared a story about the former courtrooms on the second floor. As he was doing his nightly patrols, he was up near those rooms and always got a bit of an odd feeling. It was nothing distinctly good or bad; there was just a perceptible energy there. One night the feeling was different and strong enough that he was convinced he was going to find someone in there. As he approached the rooms, he saw a man in a black robe leave one of the rooms, cross the hall, and disappear. Dave was really startled. "He was as solid as you or me," he told me. He was so shocked to see the man walk out of the courtroom and then promptly disappear that he didn't even have time to make a noise. Dave—ever conscientious, and with his heart pounding—checked the entire area, but he discovered nothing out of the ordinary.

Unsurprisingly, the basement is where the heaviest paranormal activity occurs to this day. There used to be cells down there where prisoners would have been held, and it appears that some of those

prisoners still linger. Dave would routinely have to go down there as part of his patrols, and he said that more often than not he left the area much quicker than he entered it. He disliked going down there for any reason, and he said there wasn't a single security guard that didn't share the same feeling. Some would talk about their experiences, others would not, but no one liked going down there.

There was never one particular incident down there that made him uneasy; it just always had a heavy, brooding, dark energy. So many times there were unexplained noises, and not just those of a big, old building with large boilers working away. Boilers don't make the sound of footsteps coming from behind. You can't blame utilities on the sound of voices yelling, or speaking quickly and angrily, or muttering unintelligibly. Over the years, when Dave was down in the basement, he consistently experienced all of these things. Sometimes it wasn't just auditory manifestations; sometimes shadows would move or dart around, mostly peripherally, sometimes right in front of Dave's face.

Dave went on to tell me about someone he'd shared his experiences with over the years: a former cleaner we'll call Cheryl. Dave and Cheryl bonded like war buddies when it came to the energy in the building. Unlike Dave, Cheryl was not only a believer but had strong psychic abilities that let her understand and sense far more about the building than Dave could. In some ways, Dave said, he was thankful for his relative insensitivity as he's not sure he could have done his job if he'd had the same insights as Cheryl.

Cheryl is a petite woman in her mid-fifties, with a huge amount of energy and an engaging smile. She's a dedicated, no-nonsense type of person who accepts her abilities and gifts and has learned to trust the insight they have given her. There is a trustworthiness to Cheryl that is profound, and her certainty about what she experiences and feels is refreshing.

Cheryl cleaned at the museum for three years before she finally had to leave; she found it mentally exhausting to be there. There were many times she could turn down the volume on her intuitive abilities, but after a time she found even that exhausting. Dave and Cheryl had begun tentatively speaking of their experiences before the investigation over the messed-up desk papers had begun, and she worked with Dave during the time the investigation was happening. Cheryl felt that the entity who was creating the disturbance was a former prisoner desperate for reprieve or maybe an appeal; as it turned out, it was Cheryl's insights that led to the possible solution for what was happening.

Cheryl too had seen figures on the second floor, but unlike Dave she saw them more consistently. The only one that bothered her was an angry, dangerous male presence that hung around the hallways. If Cheryl was up there by herself, she would visualize a protective white light around herself that seemed to keep him away from her, but she much preferred working as part of a team when she could.

Dave took Cheryl down into the basement one evening to show her the area and see what she could sense. Alarmingly, she told Dave that not only was the basement a dangerous place energy-wise, but also that he shouldn't go down there at all, and that if he had to he should not linger. This of course did nothing to soothe Dave's already jangled nerves about the area. He followed Cheryl's advice as much as he could, never lingering in the basement—not that he had before—but now he made sure to get out of there as quickly as possible.

AS SOMEONE WHO writes ghost stories, I found Cheryl and Dave fantastic to talk to. I especially appreciated how they were able to corroborate previously told stories about the building.

It's not a shock that a public building in which important, life-changing events take place, while acting as a container for massive amounts of emotional energy, would be haunted. There are countless examples throughout cities all over the world where this is proven over and over again.

When I visited the museum, I felt energy there, without a doubt. I did not go anywhere near the basement, not just because it scared me to death, but also because I wasn't allowed. Even in the public areas of the museum I didn't feel alone.

Do the spirits that are left there still feel like they can change their fate? Do they know their time has come and gone? Are they hoping for a different end to their story if they just hang around long enough? I'm not sure. Once thing I am sure of, however, is that there is far more to the Vancouver Art Gallery than what it has on display.

ACKNOWLEDGEMENTS

A S I HAVE LEARNED, A BOOK IS NEVER A SOLITARY ENDEAV-our—although it can certainly feel that way during the actual writing, late at night, tapping away in the dark, nervously glancing over your shoulder . . . or maybe that's just me.

I have been extraordinarily lucky to have some amazing people share their stories and experiences with me. Lisa Hemmerle, Glen Ferguson, Paul Busch, Lydia Williams, and Tani Shipka all deserve huge thanks for their contributions and the time they took to talk to me.

There are so many others who shared their stories but wish to remain anonymous, which I completely respect; I am grateful they were willing to tell me anyway. I hope I have treated your stories with the grace and compassion they deserve.

Thanks to Jason Kelly for not only letting me tell him all about the different stories, but boring him with all the history as well—then being kind enough to lend his considerable talents in producing the photos for this book. Thank you for helping me tell the stories in a very creepy visual way. I am a lucky man (bfbfh4evr).

I have so much gratitude for the amazing team at TouchWood! Thank you to Taryn, Kate, Tori, and Curtis for being patient, kind, and always on their game. Thank you to my editor Renée who once again used her talents to make me sound like a much better writer than I am.

Thank you to all my friends and coworkers with Victoria's Ghostly Walks; you are the reason I started writing in the first place.

Thanks always to my wonderful friend and fellow author Barbara

Smith, whose books were the first ghost story books I read. Thank you for your continued encouragement and support and for being the source of much laughter.

Most of all, I thank you, the reader. Without you, I would not be able to write anything. The fact that you love the stories as much as I do is what keeps me going.

I am sure that I have missed people; I always do, but that does not mean your contribution is any less valued or appreciated. It just means I'm disorganized.

My hope for this book is that at the very least it will entertain and give you some distraction. It would be great if it brought you some comfort in knowing you are not alone in what you may have experienced or are even experiencing now. If it inspires you to explore your own sensitivities and gifts and discover more about yourself and the world of spirits than you even knew were out there, even better.

As always, I would love to hear from you, so please don't hesitate to get in touch with stories, updates, or thoughts. Email me at ghoststoryguy@gmail.com, and check out my website for up-to-date comings and goings, at ghoststoryguy.com.

AN GIBBS WAS BORN IN THE UNITED KINGDOM AND EMIGRATED to Canada when he was young. He has a passion for history and the paranormal, and has always been fascinated by storytelling, ghosts, and hauntings. He lived in several city centres across the country before settling in Victoria—arguably one of the most haunted places in Canada—where he acts as a guide for the city's popular Ghostly Walks walking tours. He is the creator and co-host of the podcast Ghosts 'n Bears, and the author of *Victoria's Most Haunted: Ghost Stories of BC's Historic Capital City.*